5 Star Book Reviews

5-Star Inspirational Read. Rebekah Phelps uses a creative parable to inspire us to be what God designed us for...be all we were created to be. This story is written in easy-to-understand prose, and using animals as the main characters is a very clever masterstroke by the author. The illustrations are delightful and fun and truly enhance the story. You will love them!

This is a well-written book you will want to read repeatedly, and you will find new meaning with each read. This book is insightful, uplifting and encourages you in your daily walk with God. The book is also an excellent resource for meaningful dialogue in Bible study groups and book clubs. I recommend this book for everyone wanting to reaffirm their faith and discover who they were created to be. 5 Stars.

JOANN WAGNER, Award-winning author of *Sir Pigglesworth Adventure Series*

Rebekah is one of the most passionate and resilient women I've met. She walks her talk when it comes to living a purposeful life. As a writer and teacher, her words come from the heart and land on the heart. I look forward to seeing the impact she will continue to make on the lives of those who are recipients of her encouragement, insight and hard-won wisdom.

MARGIE WARRELL, Best-selling author of *Brave* | Founder of Global Courage

Rebekah has a gift ... the gift of connecting with individuals and audiences with her words, her insights and her ability to see a problem and offer a variety of solutions. As an author, her story telling connects ... offering inspiration and a guide to "Yes, I can," as well as "This is what I'm meant to be ... to do." Yes, Rebekah and her work as an author is a gift to all of us.

JUDITH BRILES, Best-selling author and book publishing expert | Founder of "The Book Shepherd"

I had a chance to read this book and wasn't sure what to expect going into it. As a female business owner who at one point wanted to 'fit in', I realized after reading this book that being the 'norm' or what others expect wasn't in the cards for me personally or professionally. This book spoke to me on every level and incorporating the Christian/Faith Based element lead me to a closer relationship with Christ. The way that Phelps used animals to deliver a message was smart. In a similar way Christ used parables, makes the story relatable and simplistic that even children would understand. This book reaches readers of every age with additional content for adults with thought provoking questions for a more personal journey. I'm An Eagle is a must read!

BOOKIN AROUND TOWN | THE AUDIO FLOW

Beautifully illustrated and easy to read; this book made me think and ask a lot of meaningful questions in my life. There are many great lessons to learn. One lesson I learned is how important it is in life to have the stone of remembrance. It should be a stone and the lesson learned should be remembered, otherwise we are prone to roll back where we were. I was challenged and greatly encouraged by the discussion notes for readers at the end of the book. The best thing about this book that at the end it points us all to the Creator of our lives, who deeply loves and cares for us. I highly recommend reading "I am an Eagle" to anyone who is wondering who they are, where they really belong or even anyone who thinks they are "fine" in life. The reader will be surprised the way it speaks and encourages." - **Valentina W.,** | WV Reader

Find an eagle in your life to help you soar, build bridges, reconcile your weaknesses or doubts, and seek forgiveness. Author Phelps' prose and beautiful illustrations will bring a smile to your eyes, joy to your heart, and great hope for sadness or a struggling soul. The simplicity of the book is refreshing in its clarity and encouragement without the 100's of pages usually presented in inspirational books to overcome pain or expound joy.

BET | Reader

Received this book as a gift. Loved it - reminded me of Pilgrim's Progress!

W. HOLLY | Reader

This book really spoke to me. It is a great story about discovering one's identity and attaining self-acceptance. The journey Goldie the eagle takes to find her true identity is inspiring, honest, and healing. The stones of remembrance at the end each chapter are insightful and lead the reader through the milestones Goldie reaches as she is discovering her identity. The voices of the critics are loud and truthful to the way in which the critics of our lives attempt to keep us from discovering our true selves and voice. The ending is so telling of God's redemptive power as Goldie finds her Boaz and is at peace with herself and her life. This is a great book for anyone to read, it is insightful and makes one ask the questions needed to begin and end their journey of self-discovery successfully.

AMY BESA | Goodreads Review

FREE OFFERING

If you would like a FREE extra copy of the workbook, please visit
RebekahLeaPhelps.com > Books Tab > Let's Dig Deeper

This book is also available in Audio and E-Book buy it as a
stocking stuffer or birthday gift!

Discover the unique gifts God sees in you.
An inspirational Christian parable for women.

I`m an Eagle, not a Field Chick

Discover who you really are in 19 days!

REBEKAH LEA PHELPS

THE
SCOTTISH
PEN

I'm an Eagle, not a Field Chick
   Discover the unique gifts God sees in you.
   An Inspirational Christian parable for women.
   Begin Soaring in 19 days!

First published by Dog Ear Publishing 2015, USA
Second Edition published by The Scottish Pen, LLC 2018, USA

THE
SCOTTISH
PEN

The Scottish Pen, LLC
224 Rainbow Drive #12406
Livingston, TX 77399-2024
832-953-4742 | TheScottishPen.com
Info@TheScottishPen.com

Author, Rebekah Lea Phelps
RebekahLeaPhelps@Gmail.com

978-1-947747-00-5 (Paperback)
978-1-947747-01-2 (EBook)
978-1-947747-02-9 (Audio)

Cover Design: Ana Grigoriu-Voicu, Books-Design.com
Interior Design: Gwyn Moores, gkscreative.com
Illustrations: Aaron Hoover, MountainofStrenght.net

Printed in the United States of America

Books may be purchased in quantity at a discounted rate for book groups, corporations,
churches or sales promotion by contacting the publisher.

Disclaimer: Places, events and situations in this book are purely fictional and any resemblance
to actual persons, living or dead, is coincidental. The advice and strategy suggestions con-
tained herein may not be suitable for every situation or persons. This work is sold with the
understanding that the Publisher nor Author is not engaged in rendering counseling or other
professional services. If professional assistance is required, the services of a competent professional should be sought. Any links or sources provided that have been used by the Author or
Publishing company, do not reflect any endorsement or recommendations. Further, readers
should be aware that internet websites listed in this work may have changed or disappeared
from the time this work was written.

1. > Christian Books and Bibles   2. > Religion > Transformational
3. > Self Help > Motivational   4. > Literature & Fiction > Classics & Allegories

Dedication

Contents

I'm An Eagle, not a Field Chick: The Story

We've all learned good and bad lessons in life. In this book the life lessons are referred to as "Stones of Remembrance"

THE WORKBOOK

CHAPTER 1

Begins with Egg-Spectations

Way up in a yellow birch tree sat an eagle's nest with three eggs nestled in it. One night, a storm blew in, and the rain came down hard. The wind was so fierce it made the trees bow down.

One of the eggs fell out of the nest. It hit a branch, tumbled off a leaf and over a limb, then rolled down the trunk and continued rolling toward a cliff, closer and closer to the edge.

The storm ended, the wind died down, the trees stopped thrashing their limbs to and fro, the birds peeked out of their nests, and all of nature stood still and watched the egg roll off the cliff.

Then a miracle happened.

Just as the egg began to plunge, a dove came out of nowhere!

The egg fell through the sky, but the dove swooped underneath the egg and cushioned it safely on his back. Looking down, he saw a farm. He knew he couldn't carry the egg for long, and he knew it had to stay warm. Seeing a hole in the top of the barn below, he headed toward it.

Swooping inside through the hole, he found a coop full of hens. "Oh," he thought, "this is perfect!"

> "Sometimes you just gotta be drop-kicked out of the nest."
> ROBERT DOWNEY, JR | ACTOR

One of the hens couldn't sleep and had left her nest for a midnight stroll, so the dove flew to her nest. He let the egg roll off his back, tucked it in, kissed it good-night and said, "You'll be fine here. I know this won't make sense to you, but this is where I've brought you to grow up. There's a roof over your head, you'll be fed, and you'll learn and grow here. Trust me." He hugged the egg with his wing and flew off.

Looking back through the hole he had landed in; the dove felt a connection with the egg. After all, what are the chances of an egg falling out of a nest and onto your back?

It was late, and most of the hens were sleeping. A few baby chicks had noticed the dove when it came in and placed the new egg in the coop.

The mother hen returned, huddled back down on her eggs, and went back to sleep. That is until the rooster said it was time to get up! Boy, was he ever loud!

When the mother hen got up, she turned around to say, "Good morning!" to her tan egglets, who always chirped back from inside the egg, and she noticed there was another — an egg she hadn't detected before. This was very different indeed!

The new egg was white with only a hint of tan striping here and there. She'd been laying tan eggs for years and wondered why this one was white? And, this new egg was also much bigger than the others. Perhaps this was why she had woken up with a backache! She began rolling it with her beak, talking to it, and listening for a response.

From inside the shell came a muffled reply, and it was enough to tell her the little one inside was alive and well. "Very strange," she thought, but she went on about her day, clucking, pecking, nesting, and wondering.

CHAPTER 2

Created to Be?

Why did the mother hen have a strange sense of attachment to this egg? "Poor thing," she thought. "I wonder how different-looking he or she will be? I wonder why this egg grew so much larger, and so quickly, while I was away." Would it be a lot bigger than the rest? Perhaps not hatch?

Then, she beamed! Her eyes lit up for a moment. Her wings came together (as if to pray), as she looked up and said, "Perhaps this egg is the answer to my prayers! Perhaps it will grow up to win prizes and be shown in the rodeos or, at the very least, a county fair, and we can finally get our own coop!"

Oh, she was so excited about this egg!

After that, the days passed, and she sat, and she sat . . .

One day, all her eggs hatched—except the huge egg—all the other hens turned out for a hatching party. Hatching day was a big deal because some eggs got picked up by the humans, some broke, and some got eaten by an occasional fox who snuck in or a snake who slithered his way past the night doorkeeper.

As for the big egg? The chick was still responding to the mother hen's greetings and conversations from inside the egg. It was definitely alive . . . but why hadn't it hatched with the others?

All the hens gathered around, looked at the egg, and wondered.

The mother hen continued to sit and sit.

A few more weeks went by, and one day, the mother hen saw a crack . . . and another crack . . . and a foot stuck out through the shell! Boy, that was some kind of foot!

"Oh my," she thought, "and why is she gray and white? Have I gone and laid myself a monster or a miracle? What are the neighbors going to say? My goodness, would you look at that beak and those eyes!"

She yelled, "Come quick, Pa. I think I just laid me one of those prize-winning rodeo chicks. Isn't she pretty? And look how big she is!"

As it so happens, the chick she was talking about was me.

Of course, Pa was strutting around like he'd done it all. He did know something was off. He went and fetched the doctor. When the doctor came in, he picked me up, took my pulse, listened to my heart, checked me over, and asked my mammie if she was sure this egg had come from underneath her.

"Well, sure it did!" she yelled as she slapped him upside the head. "Where else would I have gotten it from?"

Then my mammie kissed me on the head—to reassure me, I think.

The doctor said, "Well, this is just impossible. It's simply just impossible! She is not like any of the rest of us. She's like nothing I've ever seen come out of a hen's nest. But I guess we'll all adjust to having her around."

I wondered what all the fuss was about. All I cared about was getting some meat in my belly. It makes a chick real hungry to break through one of those shells.

The first thing I figured out was that Mammie wasn't too good a cook. She was always bringing grub in or trying to get me to peck with the others, and I knew right away I didn't care too much for millet or grain. It was kind of dry and felt like hard little rocks. I needed something more. So, impulsively, when nobody was looking, I'd pop an egg or two in my mouth. Every now and then, I'd get a chick hatching or one that was a few hours old. I always gave them time to say goodbye to their siblings. Ol' Ms. Alma Knack was crabby, so I usually took her eggs. She always had something to complain about, so none of the hens or roosters paid any attention to her.

> "The present was an egg, laid by the past that had its future inside it's shell."
>
> ZORA NEALE HURSTON | AUTHOR

My mammie was always real proud of me and defended my being different from the other chicks, roosters, and hens on the farm. 'Course, my being different also got me into trouble. I never meant any harm, and I wasn't trying to bother anyone; I just didn't know how else to act or who or what the measuring stick was.

I wondered, "Why was I born? What was I to do?"

I always felt there was more beyond the farm. What or who did the others want me to be like? I didn't know or understand much at this point . . . except that my name was Goldie.

CHAPTER 3

Please Everyone

Eating and walking were very difficult. Nothing came as naturally to me as it seemed to come to the others. I had to turn my head sideways to pick up grain, using my beak as a shovel and my foot as a broom to get anything in. This just didn't feel right, and I knew, instinctively it wasn't.

My first lesson had to be on eating—how to eat, what to eat, and who not to eat. I tried to act "normal," ignoring the chicks who were laughing at me. Of course, Mammie didn't know I learned this, nor did she realize how obnoxious my newfound friends and siblings could be. It wasn't just them; I drew a crowd. The turkeys and roosters came to watch and laugh as Mammie showed me how to pick up grain, cluck, peck, and strut.

> "Appetite starts with the eye."
>
> SHERRY YARD | CHEF

You could say this was my first lesson in eating *humble pie*.

It was all so horrible. I'd do my best to eat like everyone else, and someone would yell, "Look at how she eats!"

I'd try to walk like everyone else, and another would imitate the way I was walking. I didn't expect things as basic as eating and walking to be so miserable to learn. They didn't seem miserable to anyone else.

One day, I saw a snake! I just knew I could eat that! *So, I went for it.*

Just as I was licking my beak, I turned to faces filled with horror. Feathers stood straight up on some of the roosters' heads. Beaks dropped open. Shrieks and feathers flew from chicks who ran like the barn was on fire.

I wondered what had just happened. What had I missed?

Mammie came marching out of the coop with another hen, Ms. Bishop. Their body language didn't look good. That's when I got my first lecture. I was not supposed to eat chicks, eggs, or snakes. I was shown the grain and millet again and scolded for scaring everyone to death. Ms. Alma Knack told me, "You will not be trusted around my eggs!"

And all I could think was, "I didn't eat an egg!"

From that day on, I was left to wonder why I made everyone uncomfortable, what scared them, why I couldn't eat what I was hungry for, and why I had to walk like they did.

What was so wrong with me being myself?

I laid my first **stone of remembrance** _down:_ ***Please everyone.***

CHAPTER 4

Learn to listen, listen to learn

I thought after horrifying everyone by being . . . well, *me* . . . it might be to my advantage to reach out and be friendly.

So, one morning in the barnyard, I did my best to cluck and peck, strut and scratch. I kept watch on the older ones, those who had obviously caught on better than I. Oh, they didn't see me, but I pecked and peeked the best I knew how.

Soon, all the chicks had gathered in the barnyard. The clucking over this and that began. Very soon, I realized I wasn't really keen on hen parties. Still, I decided to try to play the part. After all, who doesn't want friends?

So, I decided to ask them for advice. Perhaps I'd make them feel I needed them, since I knew they didn't need me. Maybe that would help win them over and stop their ridicule.

Holding my breath and with a heavy sigh of hesitation, I said, "What is it exactly you don't like about me?"

They didn't hesitate for a second and began to talk over each other.

"You're too big to be a chick!"

"You're three colors instead of one like us! Look around, who else has a white head and is gray?"

"Look how big your feet are!"

"Look how big your wings are!"

"You're scaring everyone to death, eating snakes and chicks and eggs. Yuck!"

"Everyone is working so hard to make you fit in, instead of you just fitting in."

Then they came up with solutions to my problems.

"Maybe if you just crouch down."

"Yeah, lower your head."

"You need some yellow feathers."

"Yes, and maybe a hat!"

"And just keep pecking."

"Stop looking around and staring with those big beady eyes!"

"Yes, are you crazy or something? You always look like you're intent on chasing something down."

"Why are you so focused on what's around you, or what's up versus what's down?"

"You must stop this. You're very intimidating! You appear snobby, and you're acting like you're better than us."

I found myself talking fast to defend myself.

"Well, I'm not sure how I can change the way I look, and I didn't mean to intimidate anyone. I don't think I'm better than you; I think you're better than me. You all know how to peck, cluck, walk, and strut. You all fit in, not me. I don't know why I'm so hungry for snakes or eggs. I can't seem to help myself."

"Maybe she needs prayer," said one chick.

"Or an exorcism," said another.

"Yes, maybe we should take you to the lambs!"

"That's a good idea," another said. "Or maybe we get your mammie to make you an outfit out of the leftover feathers from the plucking's!"

I wasn't sure what the lambs would do or what the feathers were for, but I was willing to listen or do just about anything to fit in at this point.

"Many receive advice, only the wise profit from it."
HARPER LEE | AUTHOR

That's when the guineas and peacocks came walking up. They said they saw nothing wrong with my eating snakes. They thought snakes were rather tasty, too, and couldn't imagine eating millet.

It felt good to have someone be on my side.

I knew the chicks were trying to be helpful, but all their opinions only made matters worse. Now, I was really confused.

In the end, I decided the guineas and peacocks didn't have to live in the coop like I did, so I'd just follow the chicks' advice. But I had to admit, what they said piqued my interest. Secretly, I was thrilled to hear I was not the only one who liked snake on the menu!

And I would fit in. I would!

Though, I wasn't too sure how long I could stick with eating millet.

*I laid down <u>my second</u> **stone of remembrance**: **Learn to listen in order to listen to learn.**

I didn't realize at the time you don't apply all that you hear to *yourself.* That lesson came later.

CHAPTER 5

Pleasing Others Doesn't = Acceptance

The best idea the chicks had come up with was for me to look like them, so I went to my mammie and asked her what she thought about making a suit for me.

Mammie was excited, which made me excited. "Why, of course! What a great idea. Then you'll look exactly like everyone else and fit right in. And maybe you'll start to act right, too."

I could hardly wait to look like everyone else! I imagined how that was going to feel. I daydreamed about fitting in, and it helped me forget about what *I* liked, like *snake* for dinner.

We began collecting feathers from the plucking's the humans left behind. None of the others wanted to help gather them, but I didn't care. I was willing to do it all by myself if it would make a difference in how I was treated around the farm. Anyway, I hoped they'd be looking over their wings and seeing how hard I was trying. Surely, that was also worth something!

Mammie worked all day on my new chick suit, and I went to sleep that night with great anticipation of what I'd look like by the next day.

I was up before the rooster crowed. I stood over Mammie, staring until she opened her eyes. She just had to finish my hat, and soon I'd be just like them. I wanted so badly for this day to be a new start. I didn't even want to go outside to peck for breakfast until I was in my new suit.

Now, to pull this off, Mammie also had to make a grayish sleeve-type thing that slipped over my beak and attached to a beautiful red hat perched on top of my head and topped off by a scarf that went under my neck. I looked like I had shopped at the same coop as everyone else and never left the farm!

Before she let me strut outside, Mammie warned me, "If you stretch out those big, bulky wings of yours, you'll probably pop the zipper, and then I'll have mending to do."

"You wouldn't worry so much about what others think of you if you realized how little they do."
ELEANOR ROOSEVELT | FIRST LADY

The suit had shorter wings built onto it, and I crammed my big old floppy wings inside them. Now they were hidden. I didn't have to worry about flying, but I was going to have to remember not to spread my wings. Besides, the other chicks usually mistook my movements, and it intimidated them. I sure didn't want to do that. On top of that, Mammie had worked so hard to help, and I didn't want to disappoint her either. She had made the suit a little long and fluffy-haired, so the feathers covered my white collar around my head and my feet. Now they

wouldn't be so noticeable. She had thought of everything!

I asked Mammie, "Do you think this is too fancy? I don't want them to think my hat or feathers are nicer than theirs. They already think I'm snooty because of the way I look. That's what they called me."

Ma reassured me, "No, it's not too fancy. You look darling. Now, get outside and peep and peck for breakfast with the others."

In all my excitement, I tried not to strut, but I did try to move my head back and forth quickly like the other chicks. Secretly, I wanted them to notice and pat me on the back, but I also wanted to blend in. So, once I was out in the barnyard, I laid low and did the best pecking I'd ever done. I wondered how long it would take for them to notice me.

One of the turkeys saw me first and said, "So, now you're a chicken pleaser?"

That's when they all looked up. Someone started to laugh.

Why did they always have to gobble up or blurt out whatever someone said or did?

They all began laughing hysterically. Soon, a few were complaining that their sides hurt from laughing so hard. One of the guineas said, "I don't think this has made you a hip chick, but it sure has made you stand out in the crowd. And not in a good way!"

I felt so sorry for my ma. All that hard work and it had failed. Now, what was I to do?

It was still early morning, and I was starting to get very hot, hungry, and well . . . smelly. I got an idea.

Perhaps they'd be impressed by my ability to fly! Yes, I would try that.

I began running a bit and tried to spread my wings. That's when I remembered Mammie saying she'd have to mend the suit if I did. Trying to stop, I fell flat on my beak, rolling and flipping and landing on my back. Well, shucks! I felt like I was all tied up . . . inside.

When I landed, my new outfit burst and feathers went flying. At least I still had my hat and scarf on.

Then, I saw something.

The chicks were howling with glee, but what drowned out their laughter for me was the thing that caught my eye high above!

Something was soaring. And that something looked a lot like me! I just lay there, absorbed in what I saw, wondering if I were dreaming.

And I wasn't sure who had fooled whom with this stupid idea. I suppose, first and foremost, I had fooled myself.

My third **stone of remembrance**: **Pleasing others doesn't equal acceptance.**

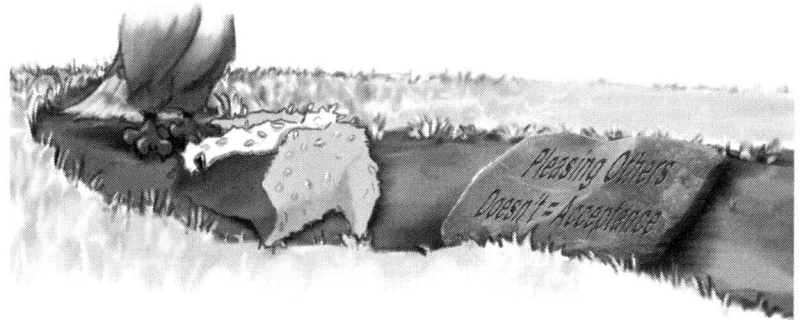

CHAPTER 6

Outfox the fox!

I definitely had not been hurt by that fall. Actually, I was even better than before, because I had a name for what was soaring up there!

At the sight of him, everyone went running, and my feathers weren't the only ones flying. They were all screaming, "Take cover! Danger! *Eagle!*"

It scared their tail feathers off. As for me, I was simply captivated. It kept circling me and soaring. *How beautiful that was!*

The turkeys and guineas got in on the mission to rescue me. They thought I had been knocked out and was about to get picked up by the eagle. They kept screaming, "Get up, Goldie! Get to the barn!"

To my surprise, they cared after all. I rolled my eyes and thought, "Hearing that was worth the tumble!"

I didn't know why, but I wasn't afraid, and I decided I wasn't going to run just because the others were.

My father shouted, "Goldie, are you dumb as a stick?"

Mammie screamed, "Goldie, don't you see that eagle?"

I said, "No, Papa Blunt, I'm fascinated, and I'd love to talk to that, um . . . eagle."

At that, everyone screeched in horror. "*Talk* to the eagle?"

That's when my sister, Sarcasm, said to everyone, "Who does she think she is?"

Ma dashed over to me—now that the eagle was out of sight—and said, "Poor darling, she's hurt her head. Honey, eagles *eat* chickens. Now, come inside with us."

I ran farther from the coop, though, and said, "No, Ma, really. I'm really interested in this . . . eagle. I want to see if he comes back."

Before anyone could stop me, I shook my wings loose of the suit, flapped and flapped . . . and flew up to the barn roof!

When I got up there, I looked down on the chicks, still scattered and peeping all around, and I thought about what I'd just done—my first real flight. It had come naturally.

"Curiosity will conquer fear even more than bravery will."
JAMES STEPHEN | AUTHOR

Then, it began to rain. I found it refreshing to my weary heart and worn out feathers.

I stayed on top of the barn, even though the rain continued to fall.

Next to the barn was a tree, and in the tree was a snake. He seemed like he had been watching me. "Who are you?" I asked.

He said his name was Doom'n Gloom.

Why are you looking at me like that?" I ventured.

He laughed. "Stop asking so many questions. Stop pondering and daydreaming. You've been told what to do. Go play and go peck. Why are you so worried about what you're supposed to be? Is anyone else wrapped around the axle about this? Is anyone else asking about destiny, or wanting to eat things they aren't supposed to?"

> "The fox changes his fur but not his habits."
>
> ANONYMOUS

My head dropped in shame. I realized he was right.

Just as he said, "You're making life too big of a deal—" I spotted a fox heading into the barn, and my attention was on him. Those words were the last thing I heard because, at that moment, I realized I was starving!

In almost the same instant, lightning bolts struck near the barn, and the thunder shook me from the rooftop. Without even thinking, I stretched my wings and just sort of *soared* into dinner.

A little while later, as I licked my talons, six beady tattletale eyes were looking at me, peering around the barn door. Three chicks were staring, open-mouthed. One was my other sister, Control who yelled, "I'm tellllling. Mammmmmie!"

"Oh, brother," I thought, "here comes the ridicule."

Then it dawned on me. I can do something they can't. And it seemed to dawn on them that I was useful.

"Well," I thought, "then that's where we begin again. How can I be useful to them? This might work out nicely for all of us!"

Now, about that eagle . . .

Later, alone, I pondered, "Is that what I am, an eagle? Well, if I leave the farm to meet other eagles, all my chances of fitting in around here are gone and I'll lose all my friends. But if I don't, I may never meet one of those eagles."

"Should I leave everything I do know," I wondered, "for everything I don't know?"

My fourth **stone of remembrance:** **_Who says you can't outfox the fox?_**

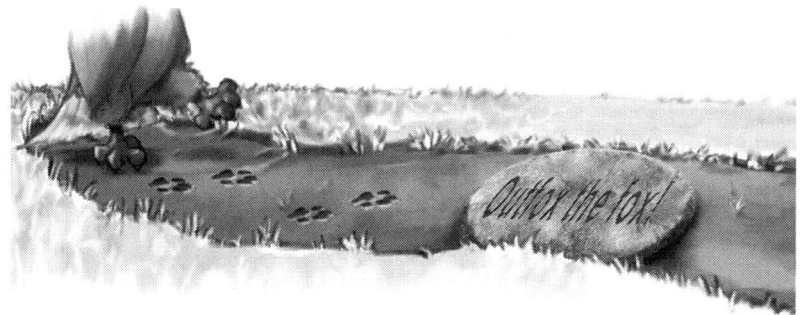

CHAPTER 7

The U, U C is the U, U B

With every passing month, I learned more about the farm. Out in the fields were the lambs. I enjoyed perching and listening to them gathering. They always had something interesting to say, and it was always so confirming for what was happening within me.

Like the day when I perched on a rail fence and heard the lamb they call Pastor Pete say, "Letting others try to conform you to their image, their style, their convictions, or their pace, isn't wise. Even if they mean well, it doesn't work out. It's just not the unique DNA God gave you. We each have to rise up, and walk or soar through our own journeys, at our own pace."

Out of the corner of my eye, I saw a few other figures wandering in. They appeared to be lambs, but then I realized, no, they weren't lambs. They were wolves in sheep's clothing!

After my little dress-up day, I wondered if they were just trying to fit in the way I had, to discover who they were. They looked a little sinister, but then, I hated to misjudge someone's intentions based on looks or my gut feelings since I couldn't seem to trust either.

Closer in they crept. Oh, they were trying to fit in, all right. They stepped right in, circled the place, and began pitching in to help by passing out snacks, sweeping up, and greeting at the door. I noticed a lot of drooling going on, and the creepy looks they gave each other as if they were setting up a raid or something.

I decided to go with my gut and swooped in. Landing on the back of the leader of the pack, I gave a good tug on his lamb suit. It fell to the ground. Then I swooped in and did the same thing to another, and another.

> "As a man thinketh in his heart, so is he."
>
> KING JAMES BIBLE
> PROVERBS 23:7

At the last one, I couldn't resist digging in since, by now, I knew they were up to no good. I landed on his back, dug my talons in, and asked him if he'd like a back scratch!

This sent them all running with their tails between their legs.

It was then that ol' snake, Mr. Doom'n Gloom, showed up again. I was discovering a pattern. I knew I could count on him for a little dose of ridicule, despair, and condemnation.

He said, "Hmm . . . this worked out fine this time, but you could have caused a lot of trouble and harm to those lambs if you'd misjudged. You just need to mind your own business."

I told him I was going to digest that information, and that's when I decided to have him for lunch!

Pastor Pete, well, he just couldn't thank me enough. That made the way smoother and opened the door for me to ask him for a little advice.

I explained about my different tastes and interests, how I wanted to break away from the chickens who meant well but tried to conform me into their image. Was I wrong to want to be myself, even though I wasn't too sure who that was yet? Or was I being stubborn by hunting and fishing? If I was, I really did want to change. I just didn't know where to start, how to start, why I was going to change, or if it was truly necessary. It seemed to me being a chicken shouldn't be *this* hard, and I didn't understand who or what the measuring stick was.

Pastor Pete was a great listener. He encouraged me to be *me*, and he said, "The object of your dreams and desires may not exist yet, but before it does, you'll have a vision of that dream. Don't get discouraged or give up! Part of your growth comes in your discovery. Exercise the gifts, talents, and abilities you know you have, and more will develop. Understanding will come. Just fly at your own pace."

When I left the field that day, I was not too sure what his words meant to me, exactly. But I knew I already had a vision and dream—and that was to soar.

<u>My **stone of remembrance**</u>: *The you you see is the you you be!*

CHAPTER 8

You can't laugh too much

The last meeting of my barnyard friends hadn't gone very well. Maybe I was setting myself up for more punishment, but I decided to go again and take a different approach.

This time, I would play detective and discover a few facts. I wanted to know what they remembered, if anything, about my hatching day. And who better to ask than those who were around *in the beginning*?

Although I'd discovered I definitely did not like hen parties, I decided to throw one. If I could get everyone talking and reminiscing, then maybe I'd discover if they had important memories about my hatching day. And so, I told everyone to come with a memory to share about someone. I even invited Mammie and Pa.

Sassy, the turkey, spoke up first. He started us all laughing about the time when the rooster, Madison (who liked to be

called *Madison Fontaine*—he was full of feathers), got all mixed up between the sunrise and the bright night. The moon seemed so large and made the night so bright that when Madison woke up, he thought it was morning. "And woke us all up with his *cock-a-doodle-doooo!*"

We all laughed, even Madison . . . *Fontaine.*

Madison Fontaine said, "Oh yeah . . . you think that's funny? Do you remember when the humans came out and began gathering turkeys for their yearly feast? We all know Snitch hides in the chicken coops!"

Faithful, the rabbit, said, "It is funny, but that's also pretty smart. Snitch is the oldest turkey on the farm! And speaking of coops, does everyone remember when some of the hens walked in and scolded Goldie for terrorizing Adaptable, the duck? Everyone was running around, especially Adaptable. She was outta there, and I don't think she's ever been back in the coop!"

> "As soap is to the body, so laughter is to the soul."
> A JEWISH PROVERB

Even I laughed, but I did kind of feel sorry for Adaptable, too. Everything scared her.

Adaptable said in her funny stuttering little voice, "Yeah, I was *almost* da-da-duck soup!"

Mocker, the snake, hissed sarcastically, "And speaking of coops, food, and Goldie—which always seem to go together—it was Goldie who snuck an egg and ate it right after she was born! Seems from the beginning, Goldie has been sneaking around. Even before she hatched!"

Instead of this annoying me, it piqued my interest, and I said,

"What do you mean, Mocker, '**before** I hatched?'"

"Well," Mocker said, "most of us know you aren't part of this crowd. You were laid down in the coop by a dove."

That's when my Ma and Pa fainted.

Oh boy, this may have just ended a good time, but I had to know what he was trying to get at, especially about the dove.

I said, "What dove? Who was he?"

That's when Squawk, Squeal, and Singer, two other roosters and a hen, spoke up. "Yes, we were there also that night. We remember!"

I noticed Mocker gloating. Clearly, he thought he was stirring the pot, pitting us for a fight. But what he didn't know was he had fallen perfectly into my plan! This was turning out better than anticipated. I decided to look at him with new eyes from now on. What was meant for harm and torment, I would allow to become useful, insightful information I could use to my advantage.

Singer clucked, "I don't know who the dove is, but I see him every now and then on the farm. Sometimes he sits and gently coos in the Olive tree. I saw him that night at the top of the roofline where it opens. He flew in and laid you in the coop."

Squeal added, "Yes, and when you were born, I remember the hen party. Your Ma was shocked at the size of your feet, your colors, and how big those wings were! Everyone laughed. Me included."

I was listening with great delight and interest.

Squawk said, "My dad was on duty that night. I saw the dove, too." He laughed and said, "Hey, Goldie, maybe that's why you're so gutsy and not a normal chicken, eating up a fox and always looking up instead of down!"

Mocker smiled and hissed, "Yes, perhaps you don't really . . . belong. You just *landed* here!"

He was implying I was an accident, but I knew better. This was intentional and took planning on the doves part.

Pastor Pete, the lamb, said, "Oh, she belongs. We all belong, or we wouldn't be here. However, we all have different purposes. And it's sometimes hard to deal with someone who isn't just like you. But we learn our greatest lessons and grow, in and through, our most difficult times."

That's when Faithful, the rabbit, and Primper, the peacock, noticed the dove.

"There he is!" they exclaimed together.

"Hey, what's your name?" Primper asked.

"Nissi," said the dove. "I Am, Nissi. And yes, I Am The Way Goldie got into the coop that night."

And then he flew off, just like that.

Oh, my. This opened my eyes, dropped a pit in my stomach, and left questions in my head. From that moment on, I vowed to keep my eyes open for that dove, Nissi.

I had a lot more questions.

My <u>stone of remembrance</u>: You can't laugh too much.

CHAPTER 9

I'm useful, not useless

Sometimes answers free us . . . and sometimes they just lead to more questions.

But questions lead to answers, right?

I was trying to give myself a pep talk, but honestly, I was just sad and discouraged. Nissi's appearance left me with more questions to which I had no answers. I felt mad and glad all at the same time!

"I'm trying to eat millet," I reasoned, "but *I'm starving* and getting sick. I just can't seem to make myself stop eating meat, no matter how much I try. I do the things I don't want to do. Oh, decisions, decisions . . . Ridicule versus stomach! And I'm trying so hard to understand the chicken language and the calls they make when predators come around, but all I really know is their sounds and recognize something's wrong. I'm just not letting on that I really don't understand them."

Looking down in discouragement, I noticed my feet. "And look at those big stupid feet! Why do I have such gigantic yellow feet with long brown nails? And why can't I be just one color?

Questions rolled through my mind about myself.

Why can't I keep my enormous wings at my sides and stop spreading them, taking off, and scaring everyone? I really don't mean to! I'm just such an oddball around here."

"They don't believe I can see far off and I can! I really can."

They think I'm just bragging if I open my long, fat, crooked, yellow beak. Oh, how I wish I could just stop diving into the water for food. And poor Adaptable, she's right. She would have been duck soup if it hadn't been for the hens in the house that day!

> "In order to be irreplaceable, one must always be different."
> COCO CHANEL | DESIGNER

Sometimes, I think it's just better to get out of the coop others think you should be in!"

I sighed heavily.

"What I really want is to see what the others see . . . from up *there*. Where the white fluffy cotton balls are. Those majestic pillows in the sky. What would it be like to soar up there?" As I stared, I thought I saw an image—a shape—that looked a little like myself. Then the light became brilliant in my eyes, and I thought of Nissi.

I went from having a lovely daydream to being mad . . .

If I could only get my talons on him! This is entirely his fault. Why did he set me down in the barnyard's coop? Who is he to be sticking his tiny little beak into *my* life? I can only imagine where I'd be if he hadn't been a nosey little white-winged, pale, fly-feather boy!"

Just as I was getting really worked up, Pastor Pete showed up. He had brought me balloons. How nice of him! They were beautiful, all different colors, with strings on them.

When he moved to hand them to me, several got away and flew off.

I said, "Oh Pete, how did you make those colors fly away? They went so easily and gracefully."

He said, "Goldie. It's not the colors on the outside that make them fly; it's what's *inside them* that makes them rise. And it's what's in *you* that will make you soar, also."

He always gave me so much to think about.

<u>*My* **stone of remembrance**</u>**:** ***Differences make me useful, not useless.***

CHAPTER 10

Seek Mentors

I really thought about what Pastor Pete said. I got out the hat and scarf Mammie had made me and decided to put them on and ponder his words. My first thought was how uncomfortable they really were, but I still wanted to try to wear them . . . or did I? I really had the desire to fly around the farm, but I'd only be called names if I did. Perhaps even a few names I hadn't heard yet.

On the one hand, there were so many problems I had to work out to live here, and I wasn't sure I could ever fix them.

And on the other hand, if I left the farm, the turkeys would gobble that right up and call me *a chicken* for not staying. But they wouldn't call me a chicken if I did stay. I laughed and thought it was ironic!

"I'm just a misfit . . . or am I?" I wondered. "The others on the farm think they know me, but they don't. For that matter, how could they? Do I even know myself?"

I had to stop thinking.

What I did know for sure was that I was starving. As I passed the pond, I saw a *fish!*

I flew over and scooped the fish up while wearing the hat Mammie made me. Oh boy, it was now soaked and drooping and hanging lopsided on my head.

The fish was so delicious, but at the same time, I couldn't help but think, "Why do I want to eat fish?! Chickens don't eat fish!"

> "No matter how wise or accomplished we grow to be, we all need someone out in front of us, clearing the path up ahead."
> CHANCE SCOGGINS
> AUTHOR & COACH

That's when I turned around and, to my surprise, in the tree over the pond I saw an eagle! Eating *fish!*

The eagle stared at me, looking startled and confused, and he said, "What's wrong with you? Were you raised in a barn or something?"

I replied excitedly, "Why, yes! How did you know?"

He laughed. "What are you doing with that goofy hat and scarf on? You look like a wet chicken, a half-starved one, at that!"

I was too excited to feel embarrassed. I asked, "Where were you raised?"

He answered, "Near mountains, rivers, and valleys, of course." He laughed again. "Who educated you, *a chicken*?"

I felt so proud. "Why, yes! How did you know that?"

He laughed hysterically, and I thought, "I didn't know I was so funny!"

Then he said, "I was educated by nature . . . and by another eagle." He laughed more and asked, "You really were raised by a bunch of chickens? You're not kidding?"

My good humor started to leave. "Well, no . . ."

He replied, "That's like being raised in the city! Our nests aren't crowded. I ate my siblings, so there was plenty for me growing up."

I gasped, "*What?!* You ate your brothers and sisters?"

> "The greatest good you can do for another is not just to share your riches, but to reveal to him his own."
> BENJAMIN DISRAELI
> PRIME MINISTER OF THE UK

I just stared. He must have noticed the bewildered look on my face because he said, "Well, of course. Only the strong survive! Somebody has to eat someone. Better me than them! Don't you realize, stupid, *we* are at the top of the food chain, not the bottom . . . like chickens?" He turned over on his back with his feet up in the air, laughing, and said, "We eat food; they *are* food! Girl, you're missing class!"

I said, "What do you mean by *we*?"

He looked at me like I had four wings and a chicken head.

Actually, I guess I did, so I pulled off my silly wet hat.

He jumped down, walked around in a circle chuckling, and said, "You know, lady, certain things about you are the same. You have the same eyes . . ."

He came close, staring into my eyes. "Same size . . ."

He stopped and stood closely next to me. "And yeah . . ." he picked up one of my wings, "yeah, . . . the same wingspan."

He looked down at my feet, put his next to mine, and added, "Yep, same talons. But you're a puzzle! You just don't fit in, and you weren't educated in the same place.

Boy, nurture really messed you up!"

I felt like I was going to cry. I'd never cried before. *He did look like me!* I'd never seen an eagle this close before. I had only seen that one up in the sky and had wanted to be there, too. But I didn't know how they got so high.

"Boy," I thought, "I really am in the wrong place. But how do I fly the coop? I'm just stuck, doomed to failure. This doesn't seem fair. Did that Nissi hate me? Why? Did I do something wrong before I even hatched for him to set me down in that coop?" Then I thought, "How could I have? I wasn't here to do anything right or anything wrong for someone to love me or hate me."

My head was spinning, and I realized the eagle was shouting at me. In his shouting, the last thing I heard was his name: Type-A.

Type-A said screaming, "HEY! HEY, are you okay? Anybody home? Oh, forget it. This is too much."

And then he just flew off. The last thing I heard him say as he shook his head was, "You need mentors!"

"Oh, wow, look at him," I thought. "He just glided across the pond and began soaring like it was nothing!"

And then I wondered, "What are mentors?"

I felt so stunned and so excited. I knew I looked like that eagle. I knew I wanted to soar and seek mentors, but first I needed to find out what they are!

*My **stone of remembrance**: **Seek mentors.***

CHAPTER 11

Face fear to overcome

I think the worst day of your life can end up being the best day. By this point, I'd learned I must treat yesterday as an obstacle to overcome instead of a stumbling block to cause me to quit. Looking back, I could see that I'd had a lot of bad days. What I remembered was that each time I thought one day was the worst, another would come along and be even worse, so the current worst always took the place of the previous worst.

I decided that, from then on, when I had a bad day, I was going to tell myself, "Don't worry; this isn't the worst day of your life . . . that's yet to come!" So, I'd wait to worry about that day when it arrived and try to pull a lesson out of today. Then, I'd do it all over again. I've never liked math, but that seemed to add up and make sense to me.

Although I was scared to death to make the changes I needed to make in my life, I also realized I was scared not to. I was sure I wouldn't be liked very much if I left, but I hadn't been liked very much anyway. I imagined the turkeys would step up to the plate to gobble up what I had to say. They always had, and I was sure if things were going to change for me, I was going to have to be the one to change. Despite the potential consequences of not having any friends and possibly having to leave the farm, I spoke up.

And so, with a huge lump in my throat and hoping my voice wouldn't crack, I decided to call a meeting and fill the others in on my plan, though I wasn't exactly sure what my plan was at that moment.

I just knew I had to go.

> "There is no illusion greater than fear."
> LAO TZU
> CHINESE PHILOSOPHER

Everyone was very nice about gathering. We stood in silence for a little while, then I took off my hat and scarf and said, "Mammie, I really appreciate you making me this hat and scarf, and I know you spent a lot of time on them, but I won't be wearing them anymore, or the feather suit. I also really appreciate everyone trying to help me discover who I am . . . but there are too many things I find uncomfortable and not to my liking."

I heard Sassy, my sister, sneer to one of the turkeys, "I told you she was an elitist."

I took a deep breath and went on. "I've decided I'm going to spread my wings, fly around the farm, and eat what I'm hungry for!"

Then I thought, "Oh my lands, did I just say what I think I said?"

I quickly tried to retract and say, "THAT isn't what I meant to say!"

Everyone looked at each other. Silence fell like the dead of night. Squeal, one of the turkeys, said angrily, "So, who's for dinner?"

I said hurriedly, "No, I'm not warning you, and my intent is not to eat you!" Oh geez, now I really felt like sticking my talon in my mouth and chewing my own foot off.

Squawk, another of the turkeys, said, "You're famous for saying *that's not your intent* . . . and then you do it!"

I knew he was right.

I decided if I am right, I have no reason to defend myself, and if I'm wrong, I have no reason to defend myself. I'll just stay silent and not make any promises I might not be able to keep.

I just hurried on to say, "Mammie and Papa Blunt, I know you've wanted me to mate with a rooster, settle down, and have some chicks, but I just can't. I'm simply not attracted to any of the roosters, and frankly, they aren't attracted to me. I really want to lock talons, soar, and live in a tree. And that doesn't interest them at all!"

Madison Fontaine chimed in, "That's for sure! She's too mouthy, and can you imagine what she'd be serving me for dinner? Fish or fox!"

Everyone laughed, and another chick added, "I can just see you trying to climb a tree, Madison!"

Then, I announced, "I actually have a desire to mate with only one mate, and the roosters like having many hens. So, I've decided to build my nest in a yellow birch tree. I don't know why I want to do this, but I enjoy being up in trees, and so that's what I'm going to do. You'll see me begin to gather sticks, leftover corn husks, and moss."

Of course, they all laughed. Pa said, "Are you just dumb as a stick, Goldie?" I really didn't like Pa saying that, but it always made me laugh inside because I always pictured a stick with eyes, wings, and talons.

Then I thought, "Well, no, I know *I'm not a stick*!" At least I knew that much.

Everyone erupted with laughter. "Gather s*ticks?!* One mate?!"

One of the chicks, Bully, began pushing me and said, "How uncomfortable!

I backed up as he pushed.

He continued, but you'll see. You're going to hate that, and then you'll be back to the coop soon, begging us to take you in *and we won't*!"

One of the guineas jumped in. "I didn't know you could build and decorate!"

That brought a roar of laughter, at my expense, of course.

I said quietly, "I want to meet other birds that look like me. In fact, I did meet another bird who looked just like me! I just didn't tell you all. I thought maybe he'll come back if I have my own nest."

I was in this far, so I decided to announce I would be putting away my binoculars and using the vision I already had. The binoculars seemed to mess up my eyesight, and I did just fine without them. Besides, I only used them to try to convince someone I really couldn't see that well.

Sassy, the turkey, said, "Yep, she definitely thinks she's superior. Now she thinks she's the farm cop!"

Madison Fontaine laughed. "It's show-off time! Girl, I don't even carry sticks. How do you think you'll get sticks up in those trees?"

Poor little Decoy, the duck, paced and looked worried as always. "I guess I'll be t-t-taking cover if you won't be eating m-m-millet anymore. *Who* w-w-will you be eating?"

I began to reassure Decoy and decided I'd said enough. Now, I just needed to figure out how to do what I had said and get busy.

I suppose taking this burden off my wings had put some on theirs, but I needed to say what I thought I should.

I began looking for sticks and found some I really liked.

I picked the tallest birch tree on the farm, closest to the water. I thought it would be a wonderful place, and I could look for fish to eat. This way, my farm family wouldn't get too nervous. And

I wouldn't burn any bridges.

As I made my trips up and down the tree, I noticed Nissi flying away. I didn't care. I gave him the cold shoulder. I was very angry with him and still had no answers.

There was a big fat snake named Sociopath up in the tree. He would often curl up, stare off (as if in a trance), and tap his slimy tail when he was calculating his next devious plot. He began to slither down the trunk as I stacked the branches of my nest. On his way down, under his breath, he mumbled, "Life isn't a lab experiment, Goldie! Stop trying to figure everything out!"

I gave him the loudest shrill I could muster, which scared the wits out of him, and I couldn't resist saying, "Sociopath, you're my favorite menu item."

That made him move even faster down what was now my tree house.

**My stone of remembrance:** **Face fear to overcome.**

CHAPTER 12

Turn doubt into a question

I had to admit, I really loved my new nest! I treasured the moss and the greenery I added. It was so much nicer than the coop, but I dared not tell Mammie because she was brokenhearted as it was.

I'd have to get used to being up here by myself, so I began reading up on birdcalls and listening for the different sounds. Funny what I paid attention to up here—things that went unnoticed down in the farmyard! I was not too sure how I was going to meet other birds, attract them, or get to meet Type-A again. I thought I'd practice a few birdcalls to see what would happen, so I did.

I wasn't too happy with my first visitor—Nissi. My secret nickname for him was Mr. Event Planner.

I took a deep breath and decided to try to forgive him, so I could move on.

He said, "Goldie, I know you're angry with me, and I understand."

I snapped, "I'M NOT ANGRY!"

Well, I reckon I sure *sounded* angry.

I suppose I needed to practice that forgiveness thing a little more before I felt it.

He responded, "You see, there is a time for everything. You're living in a place of strength now. Don't give up, Goldie. You're on the right path."

I was so frustrated with him. "Oh Nissi, you'd tick off the Good Humor bird!" Besides, nothing he'd just said to me made any sense at all.

He flew away, saying as he went, "Be of good cheer. I'll be checking on you."

What kind of thing was *that* to say to someone? "Be of good cheer?"

I kept practicing my calls. Soon, a very colorful, long-tailed bird showed up.

He said his name was Chatty Talker, the humans'

> "The whole problem with the world is that fools and fanatics are always so certain of themselves, and wiser people so full of doubts."
> BERTRAND RUSSELL
> BRITISH PHILOSOPHER

pet. I liked his beak and his talons. In that way, at least, he was more like me, and he was funny and very helpful. He knew all the farm animal sounds, and I thought it was very odd that he talked like the humans. I asked him why he sounded like the humans, and he said the farmer had taught him the sounds and words. I chuckled to myself and thought, "Huh, I guess you can really learn anything you want to!"

After we'd spent a while visiting together, he said, "Don't get weary in your well-doing. Your life is just getting started!"

Chatty and I had a long visit, and I was tired. When it grew dark, I thought I'd turn in for the night. I was dozing off and thought I was dreaming when I heard,

"*Whooo* . . . are you?"

"*Whooo* . . . is your mate?"

"*Who*oo . . . is your favorite food?"

I opened one eye, then the other, and thought, "You're about to be food if you don't shut up!" But I said, "Who are you?"

"I'm Wise-Introvert the Owl." He then said, "*Whooo* . . . are your real friends?"

I replied, "Are you sure you don't work for the farm newspaper? Why all these questions?"

He continued, "*Whooo* is your family?"

I said, "Why do you want to know all that?"

He answered, "I don't. But it's yooooou whoooo does."

I was surprised. How did he know I was on a quest to find out who I really was?

He went on. "And yooooou are the only one whooooo can answer those questions. To examine these things will help you proceed on your journey, where you will find your destiny."

That really made me scratch my head.

Then he flew off into the night, saying, "*Whooo* knows . . . maybe we'll meet again!"

I really thought, "WHO cares?"

What he had said was interesting, though. In fact, these were all the things I needed to think about. Perhaps questions would lead me to my desperately sought-after answers.

<u>My</u> **stone of remembrance:** *Turn doubt into a question.*

CHAPTER 13

Make hard but right decisions

Just when you think you're settled, the clouds come, or your thoughts change, and it's time to move again. Of course, others will really think I'm crazy (or dumb as a stick) now. Won't it validate their ideas that I am . . . cuckoo, or am I more fearful of a change validating something to me?

How do I push through and get beyond what others think in order to find what drives me? And is what's driving me really all that bad?

I'll just never know until I try and keep moving. I love my nest; it's comfortable and feels more right than anything else has so far, but there is more. I still think I'm different than the chicks who like to sit on their eggs, eat millet, mate with many, and don't give a hoot about looking up or wanting to soar.

I just think that's peculiar and they think I'm creepy.

We are simply different.

Oh, I know I shouldn't compare myself to them, but I just can't stop. I can't get meeting Type-A out of my mind and him comparing us, saying we looked alike but we're not the same. I'd like to find that school he mentioned, and the only way I will is by leaving. Then again, what if I'm too old to join, or what if they won't accept me?

My gosh, I just built my nest . . . *am* I as dumb as one of these sticks?

I've taken counsel and have listened to the voices of turkeys, lambs, roosters, hens, and even other birds. I've discovered too many differences and desires in myself, and I can't seem to shake mine to line up with theirs. As much as I'd like to remain with all I know, I'd rather leave to discover what I need to learn.

Here I sit, perched above a wonderful lake. I've enjoyed eating the fish, and now I'm so nervous, I don't want to eat at all. The fear of another confrontation or of venturing out is almost overwhelming and has me feeling like I've slept on rocks. But on the horizon, I see a mountain.

Perhaps, if I go higher! Yes, Type-A mentioned living near the mountains, high up! I'm not sure how, but I suppose I'll just have to put one talon in front of the other and trust it will all work out. I'm not going to get anywhere unless I start moving.

> "Courage doesn't happen when you have all the answers. It happens when you are ready to face the questions you have been avoiding your whole life."
>
> SHANNON L. ALDER
> AUTHOR

Perhaps Nissi would be willing to go with me. Perhaps he could show me the way. After all, he set me down here from God knows where.

When the humans came out to pick a chicken, they drew a line in the dirt over and over. The chicken stayed right there and became hypnotized as long as they did this. For the first time, I can relate to how those chickens must feel trapped, engulfed in thought. What captivates them would aggravate me, but I do feel entranced right now by my desires.

I pondered. Destiny helps you make hard, but right, decisions.

*My **stone of remembrance: Make hard but right decisions**.*

CHAPTER 14

I am not, who I was or will be

I woke up dreaming about the mountain and pondered leaving all I know for all I don't.

I thought about how I compared myself to others' standards and how this always leads to internal ridicule or confusion. Nissi told me once not to do this because "it is unwise." I'm trying to move that wisdom from my head to my heart. I suppose Nissi is right; my life is about who *I* am, not who *they* are. It's about my destiny, not theirs, and just because we're family doesn't mean we'd peck on the same path together forever. I mean, here I sit, and I am still wondering what they'll think of me if I fly the coop for good.

Why do I care?

If I'm always trying to figure out who I am based on what they think then aren't I, in fact, living up to what they worked out for themselves?

I got up and paced back and forth in my nest. I walked around the outside edges over and over. Then it dawned on me: Learning to walk a tightrope isn't about the height—it's about the balance! Climbing that mountain isn't about knowing what's ahead of me but what's presently in front; and I will never discover how high I can go until I have the courage to leave the ground!

Well, that settles it. I don't care if I they say I'm irrational, if I hear "Who does she think she is?" or if Pa asks me if I'm dumb for wanting to venture out. I must go!

> "In the past, people were born royal. Nowadays, royalty comes from what you do."
> GIANNI VERSACE
> ITALIAN DESIGNER

I asked Madison if he'd give a call to everyone. I had something I wanted to announce. I was so eager, and yet as nervous as a long-tailed cat in a room full of rocking chairs. I was going to begin climbing the mountain.

Of course, Snitch was always ready to gobble up any tidbit of news, and he was the first to say, "Another meeting? This ought'ta be good."

"I know you all believe I should just peck and shut up," I began. "I thought since I landed here, surely there was someone here who had a map to give me directions, someone wise enough to help me figure out my destiny and purpose. But I've come to

realize I'm the only one who can do that, and to do that, what I need to do is . . ."

Everyone was staring at me now.

"... is to fly the coop!"

Mocker, the snake, smirked and said, "*She thinks*... You're right, Snitch, this ought'ta be good!"

Then out of my mouth came the unexpected. I announced, "I'm an eagle, not a field chick!"

Laughter burst out around me.

Immediately, I began to backtrack and talk fast like I always did when I felt like I was in a pinch or nervous.

"Well, I don't *really know* that. I want to find out. I just think if I want to develop my abilities and purpose, then I need to accept them in the first place. I need to recognize them as a part of me, and I can't seem to do that here, so I thought maybe if I left to climb the mountain, then ..."

> "Your past, prepared you for NOW."
>
> REBEKAH LEA PHELPS
> AUTHOR

Mammie shrieked. "Goldie, are you just trying to make us all furious? Scare us to death? You should be ashamed of yourself! Leaving is just running away. You won't find anything out there we don't have to offer you here. Answer this: Did you discover anything new by leaving and building a silly nest of sticks up in the tree?"

As my heart sank a little, she went on to say, "I've lived longer and pecked more millet than you ever will, and you'd do well to listen!"

Papa Blunt tried to shush her up, but Mammie pushed his wings aside and pressed on. "No, I've been quiet too long! If I'd spoken up sooner, she wouldn't be talking this nonsense! Goldie, you have no idea what's up that mountain, and what in the world will you ever do once you get to the top? You'll starve to death before you get there. You'll be cold and lonely. You'll miss us, and we'll all miss you. You'll get lost or killed before you get to your first peak."

Then she just began to sob.

As I looked down, I thought, "But I've been all those things here, lonely, lost, hungry . . ."

I said, "Mammie, my leaving doesn't make those things go away; it challenges and resolves them. I will go with the same problems I face here, but I think that part of discovering your destiny is exercising a sort of blind faith in the gifts, talents, and abilities a chick knows she has. I think if I don't keep exercising the muscles I know I have, then they just won't develop. And I'll get older and not have the strength, ability, or even desire to do what I need to do."

Sassy, the turkey, said, "Why are you such a worrywart?"

Singer, the hen, added, "Why do you need to have so much to do? Just peck. How hard is that?"

Squawk said, "You're making issues when there shouldn't be any. Do you see me worrying about Thanksgiving all year?"

I thought, "I'm not sure what Thanksgiving is."

Decoy, the duck, said, "G-G-Goldie, you're m-m-makin' your mama cry."

Nissi landed on the back of Watch-Dog, the donkey, as Watch-Dog pushed me aside with his head and mustered his first words. "E-aw, e-aw. Discovery of who you are means letting go of what you have been, taking off the feathers you've put on."

Papa Blunt ordered me to go back to my nest and think this over.

I said, "With all due respect, Papa, I have thought it over, and I'd rather wonder while walking up the mountain than wonder while sitting here in my nest."

Nissi said to Papa, "I'll go before her, I will never leave her."

My **stone of remembrance:** **I am not who I was or will be.**

CHAPTER 15

A vision without action is a day-dream

Mammie insisted I at least take some water and a feather coat with me, and I was surprised that Snitch, the turkey, wanted me to take binoculars. He said I wouldn't be able to see the forest for the trees. There were a few others who wanted to pack me up with a few worries and fears, but I opted to leave those behind. I knew I'd encounter new ones.

They asked which direction I was headed in, and I just pointed toward the mountains and said, "I'm following my instincts."

Sadly, I departed with a final ridicule. I was labeled a rebel. But I was pleased to hear Papa Blunt say, "You have within you the ability to do what you're called to do."

> "The only thing that is worse than being blind, is having sight but no vision."
>
> HELEN KELLER
> AUTHOR

Mocker, the snake, rolled his eyes and hissed, "Birds of a feather flock together."

I made sure I had eaten plenty of fish that morning since I really wasn't sure who, what, or when I'd eat again. Then, I winged good-bye, promising I'd come back to see everyone on the farm.

To my surprise, Decoy came running and pleaded, "You could stay and pr-pro-protect the f-f-farm!"

Just then, Type-A flew in and scared poor Decoy half to death. The eagle asked me, "Where are you going?"

I said, "Toward that mountain."

He began pushing me backward, saying, "You're a late bloomer. You look sickly and out of place. Heading toward the mountain is not a good idea. You're too weighted down, and you'll never make it."

I wondered what he knew that I didn't, but still, I was determined to move forward. I decided right then, there is nothing I can't do, just things I haven't done!

At that moment, I realized that a vision without action is a daydream, and action without vision is a nightmare!

<u>*My **stone of remembrance:*** *A vision without action is a daydream.*</u>

CHAPTER 16

Serve out of abundance not supply

Arriving at the bottom of the mountain was exhilarating! And yet it was scary to take the first step on the path I found there. I almost didn't admit to Nissi how I felt, but I decided since he was kind enough to come along, it was time for us to get to know each other, and I opened up.

Although I was afraid of venturing out, I was also afraid not to, and I told myself over and over, "I'm not going back."

Doubt can be all-consuming, and I found I was contradicting myself about how I feel. One moment, I felt great. The next moment, terrified.

I had a brilliant idea that I was excited about. It came from something Nissi had said, so I decided to build small bridges along the way, just in case I ever needed to cross back that way again. I added my *stones of remembrance* to encourage others who might come along behind me. I realized the way was tough and narrow, and perhaps words of encouragement would help others stay true to their journey.

I moved up the mountain, then found a lovely stream and a few fish to eat. I worked on my first bridge and a sign that said, "Welcome, be encouraged." Then I fell asleep on the bridge.

I was surprised when I opened my eyes after a night's sleep as the sun rose again. Someone was busy moving the branches of my bridge right out from underneath me!

> "F.E.A.R. = False Evidence that Appears Real."
> AUTHOR UNKNOWN

I asked what they thought they were doing. No answer came.

I yelled again. They just kept moving sticks and branches.

I jumped down into the water and gestured with sign language, "Hey, are you deaf?"

He answered, "No, we aren't deaf, just too busy for a bunch of chatter."

I replied, "What are you doing, why are you destroying my bridge?"

He blew a whistle and halted everyone, then said, "Well, it's not yours, is it? Seems this was stacked up to use for someone who may be crossing here."

I responded, "Well, yes, but I wasn't counting on anyone tearing it down!"

He said, "Look, lady, the sign said, 'Welcome! Be encouraged!'"

I couldn't argue with that and asked, "Who are you?"

He said, "We're the beavers. Most folks around yonder call us the Ethical Family. We build bridges, lodges, and dams around here."

I thought that was fascinating! I said, "Oh, I like building nests. I've only built one so far, but I do like building! May I help you?"

He blew the whistle and told everyone to get back to work and then mumbled, "I don't know what nests are, but I reckon you can help if'n ya want."

He mumbled, "Just what kind 'a var'mit are you?" I didn't get a chance to answer, but I thought, "Eww, what's a var'mit?"

I was thrilled to help them with a project and began gathering sticks to hand them. Then, Nissi put a big wet blanket on my idea when he said, "Don't get caught up in others' purposes and paths when you have your own to walk."

> "Never get so busy making a living that you forget to make a life."
> ARISTOTLE
> GREEK PHILOSOPHER

I said, "Geez, Nissi, we need to take a break anyway, and there is nothing wrong with serving and being neighborly!"

But the truth was, in trying to help the Ethicals do their work, I only seemed to be getting in the way. So, I stood back and watched how they went about the project they were working on.

Once I thought I had it down, I tried to pitch in again, but soon realized I couldn't hold my breath as long as they could, and I got a little spooked when I felt like I was about to be stuck in the mud.

Then, I thought I'd stack some sticks and branches, but I was told to just stand back, they had it under control. I was glad when they took a break for lunch. I thought it would give us a chance to chat. They offered to share their bark and leaves, and to be polite, I thought I'd try it.

I thought, "It can't be any worse than millet."

I heard Nissi whisper, "You don't eat bark. Goldie, follow me. Let's be about our business."

I shushed him again and tried the bark and leaves.

Ugh! I spit out the beakful and ran for water. I thought I was going to choke to death and get splinters in my throat!

I heard a mother beaver say, "I wish your father would stop dragging in every Tom, Dick, and Harry he meets. We have business at hand to tend to!"

One of the beaver kids said, "Momma, who's Tom, Dick, and Harry?"

I asked if they wanted to join Nissi and me on our trek to the top of the mountain. They just looked at me—stunned and puzzled—and replied, "Our work is here."

When it was time to settle down for the night, one of the beavers invited me into the lodge, but to get there, I'd have to dive into the water and work my way up a tunnel. I realized Nissi was probably right about moving on, but I wasn't ready yet.

As I was dozing off to sleep, I thought of how much I really liked the hardworking Ethicals. They sure seemed like the perfect family. Everybody was pitching in and working together. They seemed to have a lot of irons in the fire and were very focused and productive together. No one was sitting around being petty or picking each other apart. They weren't focused on fixing old bridges but on the vision they had at hand, on their purpose, on who they were and what part they played on the team. They weren't focused on what others weren't or on what they thought others should be, but on who others were. They weren't trying to pick the speck out of the pepper or just be blabbermouths.

I said out loud, "I wonder, since I like to build . . . am I really a beaver?"

Nissi flew over and said, "Don't fall into the trap of measuring who you are against who they are. You're simply passing by."

When I woke up the next day, I told Nissi he was right, we needed to keep going. Although I enjoyed the Ethicals, I discovered I didn't like bark or mud, and my heart was set on soaring.

I appreciated Nissi's patience with me. He waited for me to be willing.

I said goodbye and thanked the Ethicals for what I had learned while visiting. I found myself carrying on with a long-drawn-out speech goodbye, telling them I loved building and that it's good to count on others to shore you up where you're weak, to work as a team, and to stay focused on the vision you have.

I learned some great lessons from the Ethicals . . . *Don't get so busy serving that you do a disservice to yourself.*

<u>**My stone of remembrance:**</u> **Serve out of your abundance, not your supply.**

CHAPTER 17

Don't sell out, be patient

I was really beating myself up for not listening to Nissi. The fact that I'd foolishly wondered if I could be a beaver was infuriating me. After all, I had just left a coop where I had always felt like I was in a spin and always trying to be like the other chickens.

Why was I losing sight of what I was here for?

I hate it when I do things I know I shouldn't, and the very things I know I should do, I don't. Why try to fit into someone else's mold?

Just when I was racking my brain over why I'd stopped for so long, Nissi handed me a note to encourage me. He said to keep it, I'd need it again soon.

I sat down to read it and calm my feathers.

Highway of Life Directions

Follow Wisdom and Understanding.

Stay in your far-right lane.

Pass the Wicked Way and Temptations of the Flesh.

Get off at Righteousness.

If you run into Sin, U-turn, go up to Repent, and Carry on.

Take a right and get on the Narrow Road.

You'll know you're there when the way is smooth, peaceful, and fruitfulness surrounds you.

If you took a left at "The Easy Way," you will notice it will be dry, rough, and fruitless. Turn around!

I loved this! It was so encouraging. I thanked Nissi, stuck the note in my purse, and carried on. I was beginning to have fun with Nissi, and this note connected my heart to his. I smiled and wondered just what I would have done if I hadn't had him with me. After all, I was on a path I'd never been on, and it was nice to have the fellowship.

One morning along our journey, I woke up with new wishes, hopes, and dreams. I wanted to find a mate, build a nest of my own, have a few chicks, and soar. It was awe-inspiring to daydream. It took me away like the wind carrying a leaf.

I was eager for the daydream to become a reality.

Nissi encouraged me to fly up the mountain. "You don't have to hike all the way up," he told me.

I could see it might be rather difficult to fly in between the trees, and I didn't want to lose track of the path I was on. Besides, I thought, I was the one carrying supplies. It was easy for Nissi to say that because he wasn't carrying anything.

> "When a brave man takes a stand, the spines of others are often stiffened."
>
> BILLY GRAHAM
> AMERICA'S PASTOR

Nissi reminded me, "That's what your talons are for. Come on, you can do it!"

I was feeling a little testy and probably fearful if I was completely honest.

I said, "Nissi, if you recall, I'm not accustomed to flying long distances or very high."

While Nissi and I were having this debate, from the corner of my eye, I thought I saw an eagle. My heart leaped for a moment. I even wondered if that's what love felt like. I had wondered about Mr. Type-A and if I'd run into him again. I began to feel excited and distracted.

I had to rub my eyes because that's when I saw a rooster and a few hawks in the trees. It seemed to be some kind of bird-party in the forest. I found myself curious and walked toward them.

"Blondie, Blondie!" one of the roosters cried out. "Come on over here, darlin', and see us!"

Another breed of eagle stepped in my path. He was very handsome and charming. He put his wing around me and said, "Well, howdy, little pilgrim, what brings you to these parts?"

I was flattered having so many birds of feathers paying me all this attention. I got caught up in laughing, drinking, and talking, and lost track of time.

There was an Eagle at the party, but it wasn't Type-A. He pulled me close, winked at me and said, those ol' roosters think any cockle-do.

He wouldn't let me go, so I pulled away and began to run.

Oh my! Reaching into my purse, I got out the directions Nissi had given me and said, "This is much too crowded for me."

Looking frantically at the directions I uttered, "I must have gotten off at Temptations of the Flesh." I said, "I must be going now. This isn't my destiny. I've learned my lesson and must stay on my path."

"Patience is not simply the ability to wait – its how we behave while we're waiting."
JOYCE MEYERS
AUTHOR & MINISTER

I ventured out and found the road to Righteousness, just like the directions said, and mumbled, "Oh Lord, lead me not into temptation, for I think I already know the way!"

I had made it to Repentance, and by looking at the map, I knew the Narrow Road must be just around the corner. And of course, it was. Redemption is always near.

Nissi must have known what was ahead for me. I would have rather skipped that mess, and once again, I wish I'd listened, but on the other hand, there was always a lesson in taking the longer route. Nothing was wasted.

Not that I want to keep taking the wrong route or that I would advise purposefully doing so; I just learned not to camp in my mistakes or ignore the lessons gained from them.

_My_ **stone of remembrance: _Don't sell out, be patient._**

Imitations of the dream often appear before the genuine thing comes along.

CHAPTER 18

Truth sets you free

Nissi and I became best friends on the way up the mountain. I appreciated him not hounding me about flying up. I joked with him once saying he must be known as the heaven hound (in a good way). He just laughed. Nissi has a great sense of humor.

True, I may have taken the longer route, but rather than get stuck in regret, I was thinking about the things I'd learned and practiced during my . . . let's say . . . *sidetracks*.

The fact that I loved to build was reinforced, and I really loved partnering with others to help where they lacked. Now, I was looking forward to finding a mate even more than before. I had loved sharing my strength with the Ethicals and discovered how much strength I really had. My menu had been much more fulfilling since leaving the farm, and I felt rested and stronger. And oh, how I loved hunting! I'd learned to trust my own vision, discernment, and ability to hear inner guidance—and just how good that guidance really is.

I now trusted my own discernment, and when I saw things for what they were, I knew to just leave them at that . . . *and* to walk away sooner rather than later if need be.

As I was mulling over these things, I found myself—guess where.

Yes, on top of the mountain!

> "The secret to happiness is freedom — and the secret to freedom is courage."
>
> THUCYDIDES
> GREEK HISTORIAN B.C.

I laughed out loud and said to Nissi, "Oh my, look where we are! Now that I'm finally here, I'm confronted with whether I am really ready to be on top."

Looking around, I shouted in excitement, "Come see, Nissi! Look at that! Did you ever imagine this? Look at that horizon. We've made it in time to see a beautiful sunset."

Nissi was excited for me and murmured happily, "Yes, I did imagine it . . . on the third day."

I wasn't too sure what that meant, and I wasn't eager to stop and ask.

Nissi seemed to know what was in my heart before I did. He said, "Now, don't let doubt take you over. You came this far, and you can do it!"

I said, "Oh, Nissi, I'm not doubting. I'm simply caught up in the beauty of it all. It's so majestic! But I will say I'm not so sure

I'm talented enough to soar out there, and I don't have to do it this evening. I mean, perhaps I've come as far as I should. Perhaps it's just a very exquisite, inspiring dream, and I've reached my peak." I stepped over to the edge and looked down, then jumped back and said, "Holy chicken feathers, Nissi, have you seen how far down that is?"

I realized we weren't alone when I heard an unfamiliar voice say, "It's not talent, it's your ability. And more than that . . . it's your birthright, your DNA!"

I turned around, startled, knowing this wasn't Nissi's voice.

It was another eagle, but not the one I'd met down at the farm or in the forest.

He flew down from the tree he was in, began walking toward me, and continued to speak. "You were born to soar! Just take a step, follow your heart. That's what faith is all about. Just believe and accept who you are!"

"That's easy for you to say, mister," I replied, "perched up there in that tree. You look so sophisticated, comfortable, and sure of yourself. To me, that looks like suicide!"

I admit there was a certain instant attraction to this eagle, and I'll also admit I thought he was rather handsome. I was also intrigued by him, but why? I couldn't quite put my talon on it.

He walked up to me. "I didn't mean to startle you. My name is Boaz, what's yours?"

I was feeling a little giddy. He was so handsome and sure of himself.

I probably spoke fast since I was also feeling a little nervous.

"My name is Goldie, and I've dreamed about soaring. I think about it all the time. But I just couldn't . . . well, I mean . . . I can't do it *just like that*. After all, it can't be *that* easy."

Then, (I still can't believe I was overcome by nervous chatter), I said to him, "After all, what would others think? Wouldn't this validate that I am really *a snob*? That I think I'm better than them?" I sighed and paced. "After all those bridges I've built just to get here, I'm glad I did because I might need them on my way down!"

Boaz walked toward me, and I backed up. In a moment, I noticed how very close I was to the edge.

He said, "Stop babbling, take off those pearls, set down your purse and that goofy hat, and all those things weighing you down. Get on my back, sweetheart. I'm taking you for a ride. You're about to *soar!*"

Laughing, I set down my mementos and began to cry in excitement. But in the next second, fear set in, and I began to ramble again, telling Boaz, "You see, it's a long story, but I met this other eagle once, and he told me I wasn't educated enough, and I was raised in a barn, and . . ." I pulled a hanky from my purse and continued, "and I ate *millet,* and . . ."

Oh, my . . . I blew my nose. I felt like I was in a confession booth.

Before I knew what had happened, Boaz pulled me up onto his back, got a running start, and had taken off over the cliff!

My hanky and pearls went hovering, and my tears stopped instantly. So, did my heart for a moment, I think!

Boaz soared back around, caught my expensive pearls in his talons. . . and then dropped me!

Flying all around me as I plunged, he yelled, "Spread your wings. You can do it! Stop flapping and just *soar.*"

> "Effort and courage are not enough without purpose and direction'. You must start with a clear sense of purpose and direction."
> MARGIE WARRELL
> AUTHOR

When it seemed as though I was about to hit the ground and become history, Nissi flew by, saying, "Don't faint, Goldie. You *are* able!" Stay in the race!

I'm thinkin' "Holy cow, WHAT RACE"

My biggest concern right then was just stayin' alive!

Boaz swooped under me and lifted me up onto his back. He began to climb higher and higher at a very fast pace and said, "You're trying way too hard. Just let yourself rise with the breeze. It's effortless!"

I yelled, "I thought you were taking me for a ride, not dumping me off in thin air!"

He laughed. "You can do this!"

Then he dropped me again and shouted, *"You're an eagle, not a field chick!"*

Falling, with my eyes closed, I began to pray.

You know you do that when you find yourself in serious trouble.

When I opened one eye, I saw Nissi beside me and heard him whisper, "I will not leave you, friend." It was then that I spread my wings . . . and began to soar!

For the first time, I was soaring . . . just as Boaz had said.

I felt a freedom I can't describe, a deliverance I'll never forget.

For the first time, looking into the sunset, I said, "I truly am an eagle, not a field chick!"

I recalled what Nissi had said to me going up the mountain; *You will know the truth, and the truth will set you free!*

<u>My **stone of remembrance:** **Truth sets you free.**</u>

CHAPTER 19

Reaching your Destiny ... It's a Journey!

Leave the Present in your Past, To have a Future

Nissi and I sat down together, and he told me, "I knew you before you were born."

He told me about the stormy night and how he had seen me as an egg tumbling through the sky. He said he knew me before I hatched, and he had plans for me. He told me how he took me to the barn below and knew I'd be safe there, how he had set me in the coop to hatch.

We laughed and cried together.

He said, "It's funny. I saw you twice before you were born!"

"Twice?" I asked.

"Yes. The night you landed on my back, and this memorable sunset evening as I watched you somersault through the sky when Boaz let you go, and you learned to soar!

We had ourselves a long overdue laugh together, and I knew he'd always be my best friend.

Nissi said, "I'm sorry if life was hard for you in the beginning. I never meant to harm you, but I understand why you thought I did. I knew you'd be stronger, kinder, and more empathetic to others in the end by breaking through in the place where I set you."

I realized I'd been too critical and harsh with Nissi. "I'm sorry," I said. "I now know you had my best interest at heart. Even when I didn't know you were keeping a watchful eye on me, I realize now that you were. Now that I think about it, it was you who helped lead me to this mountain, and it was you who comforted me in my lowest times and taught me lessons along the way."

> "Find out who you are and do it on purpose."
> DOLLY PARTON | PHILANTHROPIST

Boaz and I hadn't known each other long, but when he proposed, I accepted. I had shared all about the farm, and all I had known up to the point when we met. We decided to go back to the farm to have Pastor Pete marry us, and we sent Nissi ahead to tell them we were coming. I feared we'd scare them half to death if we both came soaring in. I wondered if they would even recognize me.

When we glided in, I could see Nissi below with a trumpet. Pointing and shouting he yelled, "Here comes the Bride, everyone!"

The whole farmyard gathered to watch us land. I could hear Madison Fontaine and a few others exclaim, "She can do *that*? Arc you sure that's *Goldie*?" Everyone cheered us in as we landed. It was a great reunion.

We thought having a small outdoor ceremony on the farm would be lovely, and Pastor Pete accepted the invitation to perform the service. We asked Nissi to circle above us during the wedding.

After we said our "I do's," we did our ceremonial dance and soared up into the sky, swooped, cartwheeled, locked talons, then did a free fall, separating and flying upward again.

Most were very impressed and happy for us. Even those ol' turkeys were crying with joy!

Well, maybe not everyone. They had gotten a few horses and, well . . . they didn't know who I was. A few of The Slobs (pigs) had their noses in the mud, and some of the ol' goats were in the rest home. Some thought we were just showing off, and of course, I heard a few murmurs like "See, I told you she was a snob."

> "Baby eagles can never soar under their families' wing."
> LIU YANG | 1ST FEMALE CHINESE ASTRONAUT

I was laughing because nothing really looked like it had changed, *except me.*

Boaz and I have so much in common. It seems he's the masculine of me and I'm the feminine of him. He always makes me laugh, and he told everyone at our reception he wasn't surprised at who I was or what I could do and said I had more courage than anyone he'd ever met.

He said, "I knew I married an eagle, not a field chick!"

And I said, "I knew I married Mr. Right! I just didn't know his first name was really *Always* . . . until after we got married!"

Adaptable, the duck, quietly laughed and said; "Goldie, y-y-you're a c-c-comedian!"

My stone of remembrance: *Sometimes you must leave your present in the past to have a future.*

Discovering who you are doesn't happen in a moment in time, in an instant, but in climbing mountains, building bridges along the way, and meeting people who are different than you are, who will sharpen you instead of breaking you if you let them—including all the turkeys, mockers, and jack-asses in your life!

Although, I still feel like the most unqualified, unlikely eagle at times when I'm soaring around, I'm glad I have learned what my abilities are and have the courage to use my wings— and I'm grateful to have found Boaz. I still thank Nissi often for taking the journey up the mountain with me. I never would have made it without Him.

THE ~~END~~ BEGINNING

BIRTH OF THE BOOK
How this "Egg" was hatched

I was waiting at a red light, headed toward Leesburg, Virginia, on Highway 7 when I saw a bald eagle, soaring above. I thought, "Wow! Look how gorgeous she is! You're amazing, Lord. I love seeing what you've created! Such grace, no effort at all for her to soar, being the eagle, she is."

And I heard, "That's what you are!"

Bursting into laughter, I did a little shoulder dance in my seat and said, "Yeah! I'm an eagle, not a field chick!"

I startled myself when I said, "Hey, Lord that would be an interesting book title!" That's when I felt a supernatural sense of silence. I covered my mouth and thought, "Oh boy, I made the same mistake Sarah did. Never laugh at God!" I could almost see Him smile, and I contemplated, "What are you up to?" Boy, did I have fun giggling in the car. I scribbled little observations that came to me about the book (the one you're now holding) onto a post-it-note. That's when this author journey began, and this book was conceived.

Then again, perhaps it all started when I was climbing out of my highchair. Kneeling beside my bed to pray (not having gone to church) as a child? Or, did it all start before He knew me, in the womb, before forty-plus years of walking through my desert, relating to Moses, hot, thirsty, irritable, anxious, and distracted by the turkeys and hens in my life. Or did God start preparing me when I wrote for my business? I can assure you, no experience is wasted!

I mean, after all, He said; "I know the plans I have for you...." Jeremiah 29:11.

For the next two years in the car, I pulled out my note pads and scribbled down things that came to mind. This book is an allegory to my life, the marvelous discovery of walking with the Lord as he showed me who I am and all the benefits of growing up "on the farm."

It's my prayer that your heart become enlightened, and you, too, recognize the parables in your own life, that you have joy in discovering (or realizing) who He created YOU to be, and the gift and talents you have!

Luke 8:9-10 and Mark 4:23

Why the New Edition?

The short answer: because the first time I do anything I expect to learn what I didn't learn in the first classroom — what I shouldn't have done, what didn't occur to me to do, or was I counting on someone else to do and guess what... they didn't. I'm sure you're shocked and that's never happened to you.

The longer answer: I wish I had met the author mentors before I had gone to a publishing firm. But I will not say, "If only Ida..." because that wasn't known to me prior. We can't be sorry for what we haven't learned yet. We learn and move forward. Ta-da... nothing to get your feathers ruffled over! I pulled up my big girl pants, wrung my wallet out, dusted off my face and "did it again."

I hope you enjoy the new edition and will watch for the children's version, a toddler's version, and an infant book!

If ever you want to thank an author, leaving a review is the nicest thing you can do.

We've all been raised on a farm

I'm an Eagle, not a Field Chick, features farm characters. Nissi, the Dove, represents God. Nissi carries the egg on his back to a barn below (representing a home/shelter) and places the egg, (known later as Goldie, *an eagle)* into a hen house where it is raised by a Hen and Rooster (representing parental oversight). The snakes represent Satan, the accuser, mocker and guilt trip expert. Some of the characters represent people we all come across at one time or another. Those Turkey's, for instance, are always gobbling up what we say, (those who seem to always be the doubt-planters...you know them, those who are a bit contrary); or the Jackasses that finally speak up on our behalf; the Owls that can be aggravating asking a lot of questions, but those questions can be thought-provoking that help lead us to answers, if we let them. Goldie lives on a farm, walking around pecking just like hens do, but has much better vision, a larger wing span and definitely a different appetite. She's accepted and yet rejected. She's content and yet dissatisfied. She's in constant search for purpose and destiny. She has siblings, lives in a cosmopolitan and diverse barnyard (representing various races, personalities and habits). Some of the animals start out as enemies and become friends. Her encounter with the wolves (in sheep's' clothing) represents people who aren't always as they seem. Through discernment, trusting herself and acting on her own gut instincts, Goldie shows courage, fear, determination, people pleasing, and a variety of other human characteristics before she heads up a mountain (on foot, representing how we sometimes take the long, hard way...but get there).

Her baggage represents just that, baggage we all carry around. Even when we "lay down the old stuff we take up new baggage. She shows us how to forgive and move past anger (being dropped into a barn vs. back in the eagle's nest, feeling forsaken, rejected and misunderstood). She realizes that our character and greatest joys come from some of the darkest times in our lives. Goldie shows us to have a dream and hold onto the vision, even if it means leaving all you know for all you don't. The "Stones of Remembrance" represent lessons we learn, steps in our life, which are sometimes realized long after they happen. Goldie shows us no matter how big we are, we all have elements of insecurities to work through. We all have done things at some point in our lives to look like others, to fit in, and we all do the very things we wish we wouldn't. We all say we aren't afraid or doubting and contradict ourselves in the next breath. We all desire LOVE.

Goldie doesn't arrive in life and then go back to the farm arrogant, but rather with a sense of humor and confident, knowing that who she is and being comfortable in her own skin doesn't bring snobbery, but humility. It really doesn't matter who mistakes one for the other. She has risen up with wings as an eagle, and soars — just as her creator created her to!

LET'S DIG DEEPER

Pluck old feathers out
Get a Bird Bath!

Author Note to Readers: This will function best in a group (with others offering insight and feedback), but I would encourage you to do it alone if not reading in the company of others.

One day at a time. It's a lot of work, but I want you soaring in 19 days!

It is my hope that you'll enjoy reading this book first for fun and then reading it again as the parable it is while looking for insight and hidden treasures. Ask the Lord to reveal how this applies to your own life.

Nissi, which is God and/or The Holy Spirit, was chosen for the dove's name because Nissi is one of the many names of God: Jehovah Nissi, meaning "The Lord is my Refuge," "Jehovah Is My Exaltation" and in the NIV (New International Version) it translates "The Lord is my Banner"—I love knowing He is faithful *over* us.

Equipping and Coaching Readers to Soar . . .
Now discover who YOU are.

PART 1, DAY 1

Begins with Egg-Spectations: Don't waste your life!

"It is better to lose your life than to waste it."
JOHN PIPER | AUTHOR

Can you identify how "Nissi" (God) is able to change what appears to be the "worst situations" into the greatest case scenarios for you, not only to develop you but to help others?

_____

_____

_____

_____

Many of us have been angry at God for what we believe were "His choices."

IE: Why did you place me in "this family" (aka: Nest) or in that job, or let me step into that marriage, or worse . . . let my child be taken, go astray, or die. Have you ever felt mad at God because He didn't make things easier or better for you? Because you were just left to crack open the shell and figure life out?

If yes, cite a few situations that come to your heart. The first few things that come to your heart are probably what you need to work on the most.

_____

_____

_____

Looking back through a hole in time, can you see yourself (literally or figurative) in a place during your life that you learned something you wouldn't have IF you weren't *in that spot,* at that hour?

_____

_____

_____

_____

Hindsight makes great glasses. Recognize ways you have been preserved, protected, and provided for.

_____

_____

_____

_____

IF Goldie had tumbled from the nest and NOT landed on the back of the Dove (who placed her in the hen's nest to remain warm) she'd have been another scrambled egg on the ground. **Name an occasion where you were deposited in the appropriate *nest,* at the proper time.**

_____

_____

Who were some of the "early witnesses" in your life that might have insight into how you grew up and who you were? What was going on "in the barnyard" *before* you were born or soon after?

_____

_____

_____

_____

What "farm" did you grow up on?

_____

(Suburb, City, Farm, Home, Foster Care, Apartment, Military, Projects, Shelter)

Sometimes our teachers show us what NOT to be. They send us out (so to speak) as advocates for (or against) a principle or cause. Give a brief snapshot of a time when you were sent out as an advocate. What comes to mind?

_____

_____

_____

_____

_____

What *Egg-Spectations* do YOU have? Write your visions and dreams down!

_____

_____

_____

_____

What Biblical scripture (or constructive thought) can you replace the negative tapes you've played in your head regarding "the farm" you grew up on?

For instance: I once felt sorrow when I thought of not growing up in a Christian home. If that recollection came to my mind, I replaced it with a new belief. ***God's ways are not my ways and His thoughts are NOT my thoughts.**** So, He knew best. **He knew the plans He had for me,** and the route I had to go to be where I am today.

_____

_____

_____

DO NOT let **unhealthy feelings** take up territory in your mind? Replace them with The Word or affirmations.

What is the initial reflection that comes to mind?

_____

_____

_____

Beliefs become living, climbing creepers that travel from your mind down to your heart. They nest in that warm place and then *"out of the abundance of your heart, your mouth speaks."* Your "unhealthy views" (or lies) will grow into a vine of bitterness in your intellect. That entanglement can take decades to untangle or destroy! We may have feelings, but we can't *be ruled* by them. Your emotions may be a gauge, but they aren't *your guide*.

What *healthy thought* can move into its place?

_____

_____

_____

_____

Like the children of Israel, we can't ignore what He has done and how He has provided. He is *Jehovah Jireh*, Our Provider.

What has He PROVIDED for you this week or this month?

_____

_____

_____

_____

Look up: Roman's 8:28, Habakkuk 2: 2-3, Jeremiah 29:11, Proverbs 23:7, Luke 6:45, Philippians 4:19

What is *YOUR* **"Stone of Remembrance?"**

_____

_____

PART 2, DAY 2

We must be hatched or go bad

"It may be hard for an egg to turn into a bird: it would be a jolly sight harder for it to learn to fly while remaining an egg. We are like eggs at present. And you cannot go on indefinitely being just an ordinary, decent egg. We must be hatched or go bad."

C.S. LEWIS | AUTHOR

Are you waiting on *something* to hatch? A dream, child, or grandchild? What are you doing while it's in the making? What are you pondering?

_____

_____

_____

Did <u>your parents</u> live any of their ambitions <u>through you</u>? If YES, are you living out their wishes or desires rather than your own? I.e.: Modeling, playing a sport, going to law school, becoming a minister, etc.?

_____

_____

_____

Have you lived out any of YOUR longings through your children or grandchildren? If YES, why?

_____

_____

_____

Do you know how to let them be themselves? Or better yet . . . **you, be yourself**?

Encourage others in THEIR gifts?

For Example: Should you see your child(ren) or grandchild(ren) enjoying drawing, you might put them in art classes or hire a tutor to develop their interests. Cheer them on in THEIR search for significance. Introduce them to outside resources. Direct them to develop and train them up.

Have you ever been fed something (so to speak) that you hated but others around you seemed to enjoy? What was it? Literally food, idea, principal, or "religion." Note: I hate religion also, relationship with Christ IS NOT "religion" that is a completely different subject.

_____

_____

_____

_____

What did you "sneak" into your life to bring some satisfaction?

_____

_____

Did you have a crabby Ol' Ms. Alma Knack in your life? Someone who seemed to know everything about the times and seasons and made you feel like you knew nothing due to age or education? How did that make you feel?

Who (or what) did you feel the measuring stick was growing up?

A parent, theology, principal, teacher, friend, sibling, foster parent, or a neighbor?

What GIFTS do your child(ren) or grandchildren have?

How can you point them in the right direction *without* living your dreams through them?

_____

_____

_____

_____

Why were **you** created? What DEEP PASSION or drive do you have?

_____

_____

_____

_____

_____

_____

_____

_____

Look up: Psalm 37:4 (HE has implanted HIS desires in YOUR heart) and Matthew 7:11

What is *YOUR "Stone of Remembrance?*

_____

_____

_____

PART 3, DAY 3

Females are taught to please others

"Whatever culture, whatever country, girls are taught to please others as opposed to pleasing themselves."

EVE ENSLER | PLAYWRITER

Do you ever look around and get the impression "everyone has talent or gifts" but you?

_____

_____

_____

_____

If yes, you aren't alone. I believe this is a very common feeling amongst people. It's either because you haven't acknowledged what capabilities you have OR

it could be that if you focus on them, you aren't motivated by what God gave YOU to mature.

Ask yourself: What do you love to do? What makes your heart leap? What excites you?

What comes naturally? If you can't see this in yourself, ask someone (safe) what they spot. It may seem "obvious" to a spectator in your life.

We all walk and learn at different paces. Some people absorb visually while others by reading or doing. Many are solitary or logical. There isn't one way to discover something. How do you best gain knowledge?

I was an average student in school, and my favorite classes were art, business, and socializing. I know, it's not exactly the 3-R's!

I loved changing classes and walking the halls to visit. I loved lunch and "networking"—connecting with others. So, in *comparing myself* with my other classmates who were straight A students and on the honor roll, I felt dumb MOST of the time. They were going to college, and I just wanted to get out of school. Sometimes, your closest friends and family don't realize you're struggling to fit in or trying to live up to "a standard."

To this day, MOST of my friends have at least 1 degree, if not 3 (including a Masters) and are Doctors, Lawyers, Entrepreneurs, Authors, Speakers, etc.

If you gave me a math problem to solve (other than adding, subtracting, and dividing) my eyes would glaze over, my mind would go blank, I'd feel panicked, and I'd probably end up in tears.

My mother wanted me to go to college to find a husband. I thought that was a foolish reason to torture myself doing something I didn't like to do in the first place. Studying and taking tests. No thanks. So, I opted not to go.

What were your school days like? What (or who) did you struggle with?

_____

_____

_____

_____

How did the above impact your life in a negative or positive way?

_____

_____

_____

_____

What did you LOVE to do when you were 8-10 years old?

Those gifts and talents have been there all along … for a long, long time. You've always desired to:

When Goldie stated: "All I could think was, I didn't eat an egg!" she missed the message.

What messages do you miss because you believe someone uttered something they did not?

TIP: Try repeating back to the person what they spoke. Make certain you understand *their* meaning, instruction, or intentions. It's amazing how "bad" our hearing can be.

Practice listening skills! Lots of relational mistakes happen because we trust that we understood someone without asking to make sure we did/do. How many times did your boss/spouse think you said

_____ and when you actually said _____ ?

Personally, I think people who have legitimate hearing issues are obligated and liable for clarification. Putting the duty on the person who CAN hear doesn't equate with me.

You may be listening, but did you hear?

_____

_____

_____

_____

Did you ever "scare" others because of who you were? For me, I was a dare-devil and always thinking of pranks, plays, and ways to make money.

At my 20-year class reunion, I had a few people tell me I scared them the way I talked to teachers and got by with it. I was shocked but found it humorous.

They were terrified I was going to get in trouble (I never got into trouble with authority), and the teacher would laugh. I have always had a way of being able to say things other people only think about and get by with it. I have no idea why. I suppose because I'm comfortable in my own skin and truly am not trying to be a jerk. Who knows, and who would have ever guessed unless they had told me 20+ years later.

Have you made people uncomfortable? Just being, well . . . you? How so?

_____

_____

_____

_____

Remember: Mind reading isn't on most of our resume's.

Be clear when you speak. Answer <u>and ask</u> questions!

Look up: Galatians 6: 4-6 & I Corinthians 15:46, Ephesians 2:10, Mark 4:24, Luke 8:18

What is *YOUR **"Stone of Remembrance?"***

_____

_____

_____

_____

PART 4, DAY 4

Respect is listening to another

"One of the most sincere forms of respect is actually listening to what another has to say."
BRYANT H. MCGILL | AUTHOR

Are you a "chick pleaser?" AKA: People pleaser?

Have you ever tried to "fit in" to have friends? How so?

Where is there room for YOU in this? You cannot please every "Tom, Dick, or Harry." Don't flip and flop based on who you're with. BE YOU, be true to YOU. **That is self-integrity.**

Have you ever received advice and been sorry you took it?

_____

_____

What were your circumstances? WHY were you sorry you took the advice or acted upon it?

_____

_____

Make certain you take counsel from individuals who line up with YOUR values and YOUR beliefs. Move cautiously when inviting people to speak into your life. They should earn that role or be summoned by YOU. Not your mate or mom! You would not tolerate someone barging into your home and giving orders . . . don't allow them to do it in your personal space either.

The times I've been sorry I took advice, have been when I acted on THEIR conscience and schedule and not my own.

WHO do you need to take **off** your "get guidance from list?"

_____

_____

_____

_____

(I know the chick list may be long)

WHO needs to be included **on** the list?

_____

_____

_____

_____

(Notice this isn't as many)

Realize taking a stand is frightening, having people or family leave your life hurts . . . BUT having unhealthy people stay is much worse. You won't have time for the healthy relations if you have UN-healthy ones taking up room, space, hours, or energy. Besides, it takes away creativity, sleep, motivation, and drains you of vitality . . . just to name a few.

What are you losing by keeping unfit "chicks" in your Rolodex?

Besides, too many "animals" speaking into your life causes confusion. They all have different customs, habits, hang-ups, food preferences, fleece, and tempers!

_____

_____

_____

The guineas and peacocks came to Goldie's side and empathized with her. Often, we are truly just seeking to be heard or understood. Doesn't that feel good?

_____

_____

_____

When is the last time you truly felt received?

_____

_____

_____

_____

Do you currently feel listened to? IF NOT, what can you do to work on changing how you communicate or standing up for yourself?

_____

_____

_____

_____

Share *your testimony* when it's relevant or timely, share *your heart* with few.

Look up: Galatians 1:10, Proverbs 13:20, Proverbs 22:1

What is *YOUR* **"Stone of Remembrance?"**

_____

_____

_____

_____

PART 5, DAY 5

Be yourself, that is an accomplishment

"To be yourself in a world that is constantly trying to make you something else is the greatest accomplishment."

RALPH WALDO EMERSON | AUTHOR

Goldie's friends came up with a way for Goldie to "look like them" versus encouraging her to be herself. Even her mother (first figure of authority) agreed with them!

We aren't supposed to "look" like everyone else! Who's *everyone* anyway? That is a very broad term.

When I went to my dad (who was very blunt) as a kid and told him "Everyone is doing it!" He replied: Not *everyone* because you're somebody, and you're not!

I've never forgotten that. Great point! On target.

What have you done to resemble someone else? To "dress" like them, etc.?

As a Child?

As a Teen?

_____

_____

_____

As an Adult?

_____

_____

_____

Have you ever been around people that have a grand idea but don't want to help "build the concept?" *Raise the baby* so to speak? If you're the only one willing to execute, perhaps that's the indication to let that concept die. You're just going to wear yourself out and be upset no one is helping!

Friendly Reminder: You aren't God, everything spoken does not have to come into being. You don't need to do everything in 6 days.

_____

_____

_____

_____

All of us walk with a distinct stride (some people take small, slow steps . . .others large and fast). If you continue to try to "walk at the pace" of someone else, you will wear your wings out!

How are you trying to walk or fly at someone else's pace?

_____

_____

_____

Remember this: You have no idea how much they _"worked out"_ to walk (or fly) at that pace, nor the price they've paid, the years they waited patiently, the sacrifices made, or the pain they had to go through. You have no true picture of what it took to get to where they are. That's the part most people don't think about.

What do you crave (or wish you were) that you are not?

_____

_____

_____

_____

_____

Examine this and ask yourself **why.** Is it something you covet or a desire that's been in your heart for years? Does it stem from jealousy, joy, insecurity, or something else not mentioned?

_____

_____

_____

_____

Have you ever planned, hoped, wished, and dreamed for a day (or time) to come? Worked hard to get to point "A" and rather than a cheering squad greeting you, you got shot with a fire hose instead?

It was such a flop it was heart-breaking? Rejection took on hysterical laughs or remarks from others?

- Check your motives!

- Is the timing, right?

- Did you receive confirmation before moving ahead?

- Are you enabling or being co-dependent? "Let Go, Let Nissi," applies here

- What's the driving force behind the act?

- Are you forcing yourself into a "suit" that you weren't meant to wear?

Sometimes "name calling" starts at home, in your "safe place." This should be a protected place. It isn't for some. *Leave it to Beaver* families do NOT exist! Even Goldie's mother remarked she had *"big, bulky wings."* They were the wings God gave her. That isn't something she can change.

What "*names*" have you been called?

_____

_____

_____

_____

Mine were: *Wrecker* Becker, Spider Legs, Skinny Minnie, Nutball, Goody-Two-Shoes or Prude.

Have you been through anything similar? IF something happens/happened it's *your fault* ... you're to blame! If it weren't for how you're shaped, your clumsy-ness, mouth, etc. List a time/times you've experienced this.

———————————————————————————————

———————————————————————————————

———————————————————————————————

———————————————————————————————

When you've been exposed to this, *you* start calling *yourself* names. I call that *"garbage in, garbage out!"*

That's why The Word says: Be careful what you HEAR. Don't listen to trash talk. What goes IN you will come OUT!

Goldie said; "I crammed my big old floppy wings inside my suit." Have you ever called yourself names? Repeated the negative tapes you have heard about yourself?

———————————————————————————————

———————————————————————————————

———————————————————————————————

———————————————————————————————

Then she worries about *her movements* intimidating others. Oh, My... that's an intense life. *Yeah, I know*...nothing you do is going to be right!

How about popping your fingers? Do you speak too loudly? Sneeze too loud? You're too tall, too big, too skinny, too pretty, too ugly, too strong, laugh too boisterously, too sexy (for church), too fat, too dressy, not dressy enough ... *scream* Let the madness stop! Don't be a part of picking at people! Just accept them for who they are, what they do, and how they look. Perhaps being a quiet example would be a novel idea!

I am delighted to announce to the world that I LOVE a bargain. I LOVE estate sales, consignment shops, and wholesalers. I seldom pay retail for anything, and I could care less what "The Joneses" think. I don't care if someone thinks I'm a snob because I own a gorgeous rug or handbag, and I don't care if they know I **didn't** pay full price for it, or it was given to me. Nor does everything have to be "name brand." As a matter of fact, I'm happy to share my "best-kept secret" shopping places.

Do you worry about what others think? Are you trying to live up to an image of status in housing, clothing, cars, being a "white collar" worker versus "blue collar?" Business owner versus employee?

Hoping people don't notice the underlining issues?

Did it come from being raised in poverty, wealth, or your own insecurities?

Remember: WHO is the measuring tape?

Measure YOU against YOU or YOU against Christ.

Now *that* is a nice standard.

I can't tell you the countless people that have confessed they thought I was a complete snob (or worse) <u>before they ever got to know me,</u> *before we ever spoke,* simply based on *how I looked, what I had on, the way I walked into a room, the way I spoke up in a meeting,* etc. When they confessed and announced they had officially changed their position, I have both busted out laughing and cried many a tear (in the past). My husband and I were in a restaurant a few years ago, and a couple said this to me (they thought initially I was a snob). *Yep, strangers.*

Personally, I can deal with candid honesty and find it amusing—even funny—from a stranger. What's been hurtful to me is the lack of acceptance within the church, knowing the above is going on, and no one will say anything. It makes me hurt for all the men, women, and young adults that STOP going to church due to the bullying and "groups" within a congregation. This is NOT the place for cliques, but it's very prevalent, and **it is wrong.**

I'm speaking up about this for all the wounded souls who might read this and need a healing touch. You aren't alone, and I'm so sorry. It's been the "big purple elephant" in the room for many of us. It's time to heal and soar!

If you've had false judgements happen to you. How do you compensate internally? <u>How do you respond</u> when you find out, overhear, or "just know?"

I confess, I've had loads of problems from women at church! Church and jobs have been amongst a few difficult places in life, but that's about MAN, not God. Keep your eyes on HIM.

When you are rejected in one area (using outward appearances), do you try to compensate and fill it in other ways? Perhaps dress down? Dress up? You don't wear make-up, or you do? You slouch?

More dangerous: Drink, use some type of drug or sleeping pills, or stay in bed?

Ask yourself . . . How are YOU truly comfortable being YOU, <u>on the outside</u>?

Then be that!

If you will compare yourself with someone, compare yourself with Jesus.

Look up: Psalms 139, II Corinthians 10:12, Mark 4:24, Luke 8:18

What is *YOUR* ***"Stone of Remembrance?"***

_____

_____

_____

_____

PART 6, DAY 6

Stand up to bullies

"We are often afraid to stand up to bullies because they appear as giants in the land but as soon as you face fear, the mask falls off the giant."

REBEKAH LEA PHELPS | AUTHOR

I'm not sure if you have a little "dare-devil" in you or not, but I do. Have you ever done something or gone somewhere others are too scared to go? Perhaps you've wanted to but wouldn't because of other people's fears?

_____

_____

_____

_____

A country, town, in the ocean, scuba diving, sky diving, parachuting, buy a franchise, start one, etc.

Being brave doesn't come because you've overcome one single issue, but because you consistently take "them" on *as they come your way.*

Face Fear!

What are you afraid of?

_____

_____

_____

How can you challenge yourself to overcome that fear?

_____

_____

_____

_____

Fear Regret!

Sometimes it takes a tragedy to realize who's for you and who's not! Sometimes it's those blabbermouth turkeys that come to your rescue!

Who went from friend to foe in your life?

_____

_____

_____

_____

Who went from foe to friend? How did that transpire, and what did you learn from it?

_____

_____

Do you ever sense people around you are talking a different language? Are you pretending to understand? Feeling like you aren't with your "own tribe?"

What age did this start?

Are you **sarcastic,** or do you have cynical friends or co-workers? Look up the meaning of the "fruits" of that quality. What are negatives and positives about this trait?

Have you ever called people names because they didn't do or act the way you thought they should? Perhaps it's time to apologize and/or forgive. Yourself and them.

How do you respond to "Doom'n Gloom" people in your life? You might also call them Nags or Negative.

_____

_____

_____

_____

Does it take a lightning bolt to get you to move, or will a light rain do it?

_____

_____

_____

_____

How do you deal with the Tattletale in your life? Don't think people don't see them for who they are. Sometimes, their payoff is simply "self-importance."

_____

_____

_____

_____

Have you ever left everything you know for everything you don't? Why and how did you do it? What did you learn?

_____

_____

_____

_____

It's not always a one-time thing in a person's life. You may need to do that several times.

Reasons: Safety, security, adventure, entrepreneur, seeker, dysfunctional family, abuse, education, simply change, new environment, sobriety? What other reasons can you think of? Oh . . . maybe just "Outfoxing the fox!"

_____

_____

_____

_____

Look up: 1 John 2:9, Ephesians 4:29, II Corinthians 10:5

What is _YOUR **"Stone of Remembrance?"**_

_____

_____

_____

_____

PART 7, DAY 7

A wolf in sheepskin is still a wolf

"A wolf is no less a wolf because he's dressed in sheepskin and the devil is no less the devil because he's dressed as an angel."
LECRAE | HIP-HOP ARTIST

Do you seek counsel before you make significant life decisions?

Do you count the cost before you "build?" Your nest, your life, your business?

Have you ever "discerned" something no one else noticed?

That's a gift. But discernment can be like fire. It can cook your eggs or burn down your house. <u>Know how to handle what you discern</u>. Be careful with that "hot skillet," and make sure you aren't "judging" or speaking when you should be quiet. If you're a Christian, cover what you see with prayer and privacy until confirmation surfaces (if it ever does) that you should take it elsewhere.

We CAN and DO "judge things" for ourselves daily. What's right, what's wrong, should I go now, later, or never, should I leave early due to traffic, etc. But what we can't do is "condemn." There is a fine feather between judgment and condemnation. How can you "test the spirits" and exercise the gifts, talents, and abilities God gave you? Put another way, how could you "test" a person in your office? Motives, a relationship with the opposite sex (if it's right for you), a friend.

_____

_____

_____

This is a tough one, and I always cringe at the response. Have you ever been attacked by *wolves in sheep's clothing*?

_____

_____

_____

_____

I'm so sorry.

Remember, wolves hang out where the sheep are. Not everyone IN church is a lamb. I'm so sorry if you've been hurt. I will say this until I die: Remember that's about Man <u>not God</u>. Sadly, some of our vilest hurts will come within the "walls of safety." Home, church, work, friends...

_____

Love covers a multitude of sins, but it *doesn't* cover up what needs to be exposed! Confront darkness with LIGHT. Turn the lights on, and what happens? The rats or roaches scatter! Never ever let anyone keep you silent over the abuse or mistreatment they have caused. Be your own advocate, if necessary, and charge through the door of fear. Never sit under a threat, blackmail, etc. EXPOSE the TRUTH. Even if it exposes *your* bad choices. There is safety in the light, in truth.

Hang onto your dreams. Those desires have been implanted in your heart by God himself. Never let the thief come in and steal them away from you.

What are a few of them?

Look up: I John 4: 1-6, Proverbs 15:22, I Thessalonians 5:21

What is *YOUR* **"Stone of Remembrance?"**

PART 8, DAY 8

An optimist laughs to forget

"An optimist laughs to forget;
a pessimist forgets to laugh."

AUTHOR UNKNOWN

Think back for a moment, way back. WHO were you and WHAT was your personality like "before the baggage," before the hurt, before high-school, before the marriage and divorce(s)?

_____

_____

_____

_____

By the way . . . Yes, God says He hates divorce. He NEVER said He hates *the divorcee*. **He hates divorce because He knows the pain of it**, He knows the ache and discomfort you must go through to get to the place where you say ENOUGH IS ENOUGH, I'm not living this way! God divorced nations, from Israel to Sodom and Gomorrah. So, you think if He won't contend with "man" forever He expects you too? Of course not! There is way too much shame being tossed on people, and it's so wrong. God wants you wearing a coat of many colors, not clothed in guilt and remorse! He hasn't asked you to haul those bags around!

Think Back: From 3 to 10 years old if you can (if you can't ask someone that remembers you at that age). Peek at old photos that might trigger a few memories.

To help you recollect who that child was:

What did you love to do?

_____

_____

What fascinated you?

_____

_____

Did you ask lots of questions? Love to listen to people's stories?

_____

_____

Were you a runner? Enjoyed sports? Actress in the making? Dancer? Singer?

_____

_____

Could you entertain yourself or did you need people around you to be stimulated?

_____

_____

Were you artistic? Love to doodle, paint, or draw?

_____

_____

Did you teach yourself things and then teach others?

_____

_____

Did you have a heart for the "underdogs" or enjoy serving others?

_____

_____

Perhaps you were a storyteller, you loved to journal or were a comedian.

_____

_____

What did I leave out?

_____

_____

Discuss a few things with a group and let them help you discover who you are.

Who you were is who you are. Work from that point. Work on the positives and negatives! **List examples below to trigger a memory.**

What did you do?

_____

_____

So, WHO are you?

List as many as you can . . . dissect and dig deep.

Examples:

8 MONTHS OLD...

What I did: I bowed my head to pray before I could talk, I prayed "Our Father who art in Heaven . . ." (the entire prayer) by the time I was two years old.

Who I am: I'm an intercessor. God created me to pray for others.

2-8+ YEARS OLD...

What I did: If I learned something, I "taught it" to others.
Who I am: I'm a teacher, not an educator (remember, no college).

8-10 YEARS OLD...

What I did: I orchestrated "plays" and "dances" and then invited people to watch . . . for money! The chemist in me melted down bars of soap (to make "soft soap®") and sold it to neighbors.

Who I am: I'm an entrepreneur & a salesperson. I suppose I should add inventor and thief. My mother was NOT happy with my entrepreneurial idea.

4 YEARS OLD...

What I did: If someone bullied someone else, or I saw "injustice" . . . I spoke up.

Who I am: I'm a confronter. I want to deal with and resolve issues.

11 YEARS OLD...

What I did: I painted and sold my paintings when I was 11.

 Who I am: I'm an artist.

Note: The _"Performer"_ in me began blooming again at age 49. I'd like to also remark . . . "Performer" has gotten squashed and stomped within so many churches. That falls under so many wonderful gifts: comedian, painter, singer, dancer, artist, actor, cartoonist, sculptor—you get it! Just love _Jesus_ more than you love "self" and "your abilities." You'll be on track, and if you aren't, He is more than able to get you on track. He will meet you where you are!

And as far back as I can remember, I always wanted to know who Jesus was. I often wanted to go to church and ask (_ok, I was obsessed_) why He put me here on this earth. I wanted a Bible for my 6th birthday. I became a Christian at age 20. I hope those examples help. Think . . . think hard or go ask!

Do you have a mocker in your life?

I find this to be a valuable person. They give clues as to WHAT "the enemy" is trying to destroy, tear down, or _sew_ doubt into the quilt of your life so you will turn away from "it."

The same is true with the voice of the accuser. Listen, you might find a nugget of truth that is valuable insight even though it's being presented in a nasty little gift wrap! They just gave you something to work on! Not all negative feedbacks are negative! Watch for patterns and consistency, examine your own heart and take it to the Lord NOT others.

For Example: My entire life, I have been hounded, ridiculed and at times hated for being truthful or wanting to know *The Truth*. It created an enormous amount of grief in me as a child.

I have been kicked out of my parents' home (or my own by an Ex-spouse) for talking about The Lord and have been in more trouble for being honest (and speaking up) than I ever have for lying. It was one of the many reasons I divorced a fake minister. I wouldn't shut up and be a quiet little "church mouse." I have been told to muzzle my mouth, just stay home (from church), sit down, be inaudible, be loving (implying I'm not because I'm speaking The Word/truth), I'm too harsh or brash . . . all over Truth. The Word has a lot to say about this topic and for me to get flogged over this issue "by man/woman" . . . DING, *Hallelujah*. Thank you for that confirmation! That calls for a *"get behind me Satan"* statement.

God is the judge *of the thoughts and intents of my heart*. Not mankind. We have no business judging each other, that only shoots the wounded. *The Sword* is to be used against the enemy, NOT each other.

It's a constant issue for me. The enemy would like me to be silent. TOUGH—I don't take orders from the devil, he will take them from me! We have been given dominion over him, not vice versa.

Now, every time this comes up, I grin. He's still hounding me. Too funny.

Give an example of a way the devil is hounding/has hounded you.

_____

_____

I have seen people in the occult manifest demonic activity and do back flips without me laying a hand on them because God moved, TRUTH was spoken, and I prayed over them. I've seen oil pour from my hands in the heat of summer when I prayed for someone and spoke TRUTH to them. God has let me know clearly who I am IN HIM. I'm waiting... I am not here to die popular, not trying to win any best-selling author awards, nor do I care if I'm a household name. I care if my name is written in Heaven. Period. I am burdened to help the broken-hearted heal and find purpose. I am restless to see captives set free. TRUTH sets people free, not fluff. Not playing church but being The Church. I'm an Eagle who will rise and not be weary...

What do you long to see in your own life? Has God given you any glimpses as to how he might use you?

How have *these characters* in your life made an impact? If at all?

The Primper (other than taking a long time to get ready)

Someone Faithful

_____

_____

_____

Adaptable

_____

_____

_____

Squawk (the screamer)

_____

_____

_____

Snitch (the tattletale)

_____

_____

_____

Singer/Performer? Someone who wants to be noticed

_____

_____

_____

How about Mr. Ego (Madison Fontaine) - Someone who insist on being addressed with titles versus a first name basis?

_____

_____

_____

Do you have a Pastor you can go to? That's can be tough. Nowadays, we have loads of "Ministers," lots of "Preachers," but very few Pastors. What a shame.

_____

_____

_____

Finally, what about Nissi? AKA: *God*? Where is He in your life?

_____

_____

_____

Look up: John 10:14, John 10:27, Isaiah 43:1, Psalm 139: 1-24, Matthew 25: 14-30, Hebrews 4:12, James 1:2, I Peter 2:4, Proverbs 31:8, Galatians 1:10, Genesis 3:15 and Luke 10:19

What is *YOUR* **_"Stone of Remembrance?"_**

_____

_____

PART 9, DAY 9

Don't be average

"The hardest struggle of all is to be something different from what the average person is."

CHARLES SCHWAB | PHILANTHROPIST

What TRUTH have you discovered regarding yourself? I hope a nugget or two from the last chapter.

_____

_____

_____

_____

Do you have someone to forgive? Who?

Note: I **didn't** say _what for._

_____

_____

I promise you this, if you don't forgive, forget ever "flying." Don't expect answered prayers, scratch succeeding off the list, forget about being at peace or being filled with JOY. You can't . . . you're dragging around too much weight.

Just as a crazy exercise, do this if you don't believe me.

Take **all** the luggage out of your closet, drag it **all** around everywhere you go for one day. Aww, come on . . . it's just one day! Though, I'm sure you'll get the point after a few hours. Take it **all** to the grocery store, doctor's office, pile it in the bathroom with you, hey . . . take a nap with it! I mean, you're doing it anyway. This "visual" could be lifesaving for you! You'll feel like you drank from the fountain of youth when you get rid of the baggage of unforgiveness.

The inside of the cup matters. If you want "your cup" to overflow . . . forgive!

Empty the bags, and bury them in the closet where they belong!

Your conscience is the first level of authority God works with or through. I'd imagine you have someone to forgive, even if it's just yourself. Start there.

What "things" do you do that you know you shouldn't be doing, but you do anyway?

_____

_____

_____

_____

We are a spirit, we live in a body, and we have a soul. Those 3 things are in constant competition with each other. It's up to US to train our soul (mind, will, and emotions). From the time we were infants we cried, and a bottle was stuck in our mouth. We wet our pants, and our diapers were changed. We wept, and someone came running. Our SOULS are MUCH older than our spirits when it comes to being trained and pampered here on this place called Earth. Some adults are still acting like infants, some bosses are! They scream, we come running to coddle them.

Some things are normal and natural (IE: we get hungry, we get tired), but it's out of balance when we are RULED by our appetites or run ourselves into the ground working 24/7. Our bodies can't keep up. Our health will suffer.

How can you work on training that *soulish-self* into being a more content spirit being? I promise you will end up more peaceful, trusting, and balanced.

This is a crucial lesson if you want more from God himself.

Why are you trying to prove who you are to someone else? Just Be YOU.

_____

_____

You don't owe them the TIME you're putting into this!

Are you mad at God? About what?

_____

_____

_____

_____

I promise He can handle your honesty and is waiting on it.

What is IN you that will make you rise and soar?

_____

_____

_____

_____

Look up: Matthew 7:5, John 8:31-32, Mark 11:26, Matthew 23:26-28, Matthew 6:14-15, Isaiah 40:31

What is *YOUR* **_"Stone of Remembrance?"_**

_____

_____

_____

_____

PART 10, DAY 10

Mentors help navigate

"One of the greatest values of mentors is the ability to see ahead what others cannot see and to help them navigate a course to their destination."
JOHN C. MAXWELL | AUTHOR/PASTOR

Have you ever gauged yourself against others? Then sat on the bench and judged yourself that you didn't "qualify?" Perhaps because of education or "neighborhood"—families, race, or even personal style? Maybe you're short versus tall, have brown eyes versus blue, or black hair versus blonde? Are you continuing to do this? How?

_____

_____

_____

Hopefully, you are on your way to stopping. Remember: Brain Train! DAILY.

Everyone can learn something from each other.

Reach out. Seek mentors!

They don't have to know or accept a formal invitation. Just watch, listen, and ask questions to those you admire.

Whom do you admire?

_____

_____

Look up to?

_____

_____

_____

Who encourages you?

_____

_____

_____

Always reach HIGHER. Jesus led a life of mentoring others.

Isn't it great when you feel like you've met someone you connect with? You may have connected because you felt as if "they were like you!" See, you do like yourself. You do have qualities you admire. It's that feeling of "aww, that appears familiar!"

What qualities do you admire most about yourself?

_____

_____

_____

_____

I love a dry sense of humor and a person that's hilarious but doesn't know they are. One of my grandmothers was like that. However, when a Type-A personality comes along and begins to mull you over, it's suddenly not so funny. When he starts hanging his degrees out it can be intimidating, when he reminds you that you're a country bumpkin and he's from the city . . . um, well . . . is there something wrong with being from the country? When she wants to work 24/7, and you just want to go home.

I can be very Type-A at times (cough, cough), my doctors say I'm a "Nice Type-A," but I can be blunt. So much so, I've been called Frank more than Rebekah, well, *not more* . . . just a lot.

My best advice for dealing with this type of person is to stand toe-to-toe with them. They just like a debate, they are confrontational to resolve or understand, not to fight. They aren't scared to express their opinions and feelings, and you'll find they have a lot of compassion and a huge soft spot. Why? Because most paid a heavy price to get to where they are. Get in that *boxing ring* with them. They won't hurt you, they'll admire you, and be a great mentor! When you approach them, ask for an appointment, get to the point, cut to the chase, spare 'em the details and move on!

Look up: Proverbs 27:17, Proverbs 9:9, Proverbs 1:5, John 14:26, Galatians 6:4

What is *YOUR **"Stone of Remembrance?"***

_____

_____

_____

PART 11, DAY 11

Wipe out that judgement

"If you are pained by external things, it is not they that disturb you, but your own judgment of them. And it is in your power to wipe out that judgement now."

MARCUS AURELIUS | ROMAN EMPEROR

What is the most difficult "hindrance" in your life that you know you must overcome to move forward?

_____

_____

I'll mention this again: Un-forgiveness WILL hold you back. Forgiveness and "restoration" **aren't** the same. One thing has NOTHING to do with the other.

For instance, sometimes people destroy trust that can't be rebuilt. But the act committed is forgivable. It DOES NOT mean you agree with the perpetrator.

I am compelled to mention this because so many people have a "fear issue" about forgiveness. They think if they exonerate, they must unite—not true. Relax, and pardon.

Don't despair. I know it's difficult. I've seen many dark places in my life also but keep the faith no matter what. You will have another "worse" in your life, and you'll overcome that too.

Our lives are like mushrooms, they grow in an old, dark, stinky outhouse with lots of "junk" piled on top!

What fear do you need to face? **Tip:** Pray and fast, then tackle it.

NOTE: Fasting doesn't have to be food, it could be giving up ANYTHING you really enjoy and rely on. Internet or TV would be a "sacrifice" for many! Some people don't eat regular meals anyway, so that wouldn't be a "sacrifice."

_____

_____

_____

_____

Who do you need to forgive?

_____

_____

_____

_____

What do you need to "take off" (literally or figuratively) and set aside to move on?

_____

_____

Who do you need to go to and state some facts or feelings?

Don't do this IF it will cause you more hurt, abuse, or bullying. If that's the case, just go to The Lord. He'll listen. Go to a counselor, PTSD professional, therapist, etc.

Remember if you're right, you have no reason to defend yourself, and if you're wrong, you have no reason to defend yourself. Sometimes, silence is the best policy when you're stating your wishes or decisions. Be prepared for ridicule.

Write down what others might throw at you IF YOU STATED: _____.

Now you're anticipating what will be retorted.

Do you have a Bully in your life? Pushing vs. leading? What's going on? Who can you go to? If you can confront them one on one, do that. If you've done that and they still won't listen take a witness.

_____

_____

How about a Sociopath?

_____

_____

Ugh, those are the worst. They are in every office, school, and church. They have no conscience about who they hurt, they are calculated and devious. I call them emotional arsonists. They love to start fires then stand back and watch them burn! They are very hard to discover and weed out. They love to divide people and lie about people's character. It takes time and patterns to catch them at work. Know one? They won't like it when you're onto them. They attach themselves to people who TRULY have integrity to justify to themselves that they are okay. IF they can't attach themselves to you, they try to destroy your reputation.

_____

_____

_____

_____

Look up: Isiah 57:14, Hebrews 12:1, Philippians 3:14, Psalm 66:10-12, II Timothy 1:7, Matthew 18:16, Roman 8:5-8

What is _YOUR **"Stone of Remembrance?"**_

_____

_____

_____

PART 12, DAY 12

Deal with Doubt

"The only limit to our realization of tomorrow
will be our doubts today."
FRANKLIN D. ROOSEVELT
32ND PRESIDENT OF THE UNITED STATES

Are you afraid to be alone? _____ If yes, what are you afraid
will happen? Worst case scenario?

_____

_____

Are you willing to work through loneliness and isolation to get to
where you need to go? That's a tough one, I've been there.

_____

_____

_____

What questions should you <u>reconsider</u> that someone has asked of you?

_____

_____

Do you ever respond in haste or anger and then regret? Of course, we all have! Rather than deny the feelings you have, as soon as you see it, own it. Take your part in a matter, but don't keep someone else's. Give examples of the outcomes when you have responded in haste or anger.

_____

_____

_____

I'll ask again. Are you angry with God? He can handle whatever you have to say. Can you turn your doubt into a question for Him? Write it down. Now wait for the answer. He is faithful. Be listening for the answer.

_____

_____

_____

I have observed that many people who have an issue with God also have/had an issue with their earthly father or the lack thereof. If our examples were harsh, judgmental, abusive, absent, and cruel; OR your heart and mind were spoiled against them . . . then it's no wonder you have a problem with the creator of the universe! He's sitting in heaven on this big white throne ready to cast you aside and mock at your pride. WRONG! It's totally the opposite. If you were abused by a "spiritual father" within the church, again, I'm so sorry. That reflects mankind. I'm praying you heal and give Abba a chance.

Look up: I Peter 5:7, Hebrews 13:6, Psalm 27:10, I Samuel 12:22, Roman 8:31-38, Matthew 7:7, Matthew 11:28

What is *YOUR* ***"Stone of Remembrance?"***

_____

_____

_____

_____

PART 13, DAY 13

Lean not unto your own understanding

"Trust in the LORD with all thine heart; and lean
not unto thine own understanding. In all thy ways
acknowledge him, and he shall direct thy paths."
PROVERBS 3:5-6 | THE HOLY BIBLE

Don't allow doubt to dominate you. Doubt is the opposite of faith. It leads to unbelief, and unbelief will rob you of your hopes and dreams. It's that wicked vine. Pull up that Kudzu at the roots.

What are you doubting?

_____

_____

_____

_____

What can you replace that negative belief system with?

_____

_____

_____

Faith is a verb . . . it *moves* forward.

What hard—but right—decisions do you need to make?

_____

_____

_____

_____

Have you ever moved and then suddenly you find yourself moving again? Boy, I have. I have felt like a gypsy at times. But you won't ever get to Step B until you move to Step A. NOTHING is wasted.

Life is full of lessons to learn. What "classroom" would you have missed out on if you had stayed where you were?

_____

_____

_____

_____

Be willing to go where you've never been, to get to where you've never gone.

Look up: Proverbs 3:5-8, James 1:6, Matthew 21:21, Isaiah 41:10, Hebrews 11:1-40

What is *YOUR "Stone of Remembrance?"*

_____

_____

_____

PART 14, DAY 14

It's not the stars that hold my destiny

"It's not the stars that hold my destiny,
but the one who created the stars."
REBEKAH LEA PHELPS | AUTHOR

Comparing yourself to others leads to self-ridicule and confusion. Comparison piles up, and you begin to feel useless instead of useful and worthless versus worthy. This may lead you down a path of jealousy or envy.

When someone shuts you down and says they know best because _____, it can be demeaning, invalidating, and disrespectful. ALL people deserve a voice. ALL people need to come to knowledge and experience on their own.

Grey and silver hair on the head doesn't mean wisdom. <u>Wisdom comes from spending time with God.</u> Even children can distribute wisdom. You may appear "cold" to others, but you can't allow others to control you. Often people use their emotions, desires, or even experience for what THEY THINK is right for your life. Check with God first. We're supposed to be "following Him" *not them.*

A donkey in the Bible spoke to a very stubborn prophet. God can use whatever and whoever He wants to use. He's even used "storms" and a spider web to teach me important lessons.

What lessons have you learned by observing nature?

_____

_____

_____

Has He ever used a "jack-ass" in your life? Maybe a wolf in sheep's clothing? A "Turkey" or "Snake?" Sometimes, those "animals" (people/characters) can teach us what NOT to be. That IS the lesson.

Think of something "natural" that taught you something "spiritual?"

_____

_____

_____

Listen, He's speaking . . .

Who you are is not who you were, or who you will be. Can you give examples of how you've grown or overcome?

_____

_____

_____

_____

WARNING: Refuse to live in shame, regret, and sorrow. Particularly, if you have asked for forgiveness. Our sin is against God and God only, and HE WILL forgive you and wants you to move on to higher ground! Don't beat yourself up—the world will do that (time to stop letting them.)

Only Fear Regret.

Don't live on *I always wanted to, but.*

I've learned the hard way, never respond to other people's tears meant only to get you to something (stay, marry, join, etc.). People will be sad over some of your decisions, they are just going to have to get over it. I don't think ALL tears are about manipulation or start out that way, but it can be that in some cases. You must weigh that situation. I have made many poor choices over other people's tears. Then guess what . . . I was the one crying in the end, and they could have cared less. Can you relate?

Tip: Look for a pattern. Ask yourself: Is this an incident or a lifestyle from this person?

Secondly, when someone calls you crying, don't be scared to give them 24 - 48 hours before you get back to them. Spare yourself drama and details. They will have a chance to calm down, go to The Lord (if Christian), or work it out themselves. It's setting healthy boundaries.

Your thoughts?

_____

_____

_____

Have you ever had someone try to *project* all that could happen (in a bad sense - future) versus all that could be waiting (in a good sense)?

Most people are so busy living in the past or future, they miss the present! It's like trying to drive looking in the rear-view mirror for goodness sakes. Share an example of a time you did this.

_____

_____

_____

_____

We do have mental muscle. We ACT brave, we TAKE courage, we CONFRONT fear, we STAND for what's right, we PRACTICE what we learn, we are DOERS, *not just hearers*. It's like working out . . . just a different muscle. What would you like to do NOW, that you might not be able to do later if you don't EXERCISE and DEVOLOPE that skill? That desire? That Hope? That Talent?

_____

_____

_____

_____

_____

You aren't a "worrywart," you simply have a sense of PURPOSE. You're driven to discover, to learn to be all you were created to be. So, go be it! Ask yourself, what drives you? What's your purpose and passion?

_____

_____

_____

_____

_____

Look up: II Corinthians 10:12, Galatians 1:10, Galatians 6:4-5, James 3:16, I Timothy 4:12, Matthew 16:23, James 1:23

What is *YOUR* ***"Stone of Remembrance?"***

_____

_____

_____

_____

PART 15, DAY 15

People should laugh at your goals

"If people are not laughing at your goals,
your goals are too small."
AZIM PREMJI | PHILANTHROPIST

You have heard the saying; "you can't see the forest for the trees?"

Sometimes, that holds true depending on the height at which you're standing. So, focus on where you are. If you can't see beyond where you are and you're not a visionary person, then focus on what you can see.

What can you see?

_____

_____

_____

_____

Don't lose your stamina, courage, or the pace at which you can fly because of what could be, should be, will be, or could happen.

Face the fear—One "talon" at a time.

What are you facing now?

_____

_____

_____

_____

Are you afraid? Of what?

_____

_____

What one thing do you need to focus on?

_____

_____

What CAN'T you see because you're moving through the forest right now?

_____

_____

_____

Have you ever been labeled a rebel for doing something you felt convicted or led to do? Perhaps even situations you received confirmation on?

Give examples.

_____

_____

_____

_____

Perhaps not "a rebel" but something else? (Snob, stuck up, black sheep, loner, daredevil.) In hindsight, was it true or false?

_____

Did it make you consider if what they were saying was true? Second guess yourself? What did that lead to?

_____

_____

_____

_____

There is always a bit of truth within a lie. So, what IS true and what's the lie?

_____

_____

_____

Birds of a Feather do flock together, water seeks its own level, and you can judge a man by the friends he keeps. Jesus was friends with sinners, the outcast, the average everyday "Joe." However, He didn't take their counsel, he gave direction, warning, and guidance. He turned water into wine but didn't get drunk with people. He led versus followed.

Be the leader the world is looking for! There are lots of hurting people looking for direction. How can you be a leader, not a follower?

_____

_____

_____

When you begin to move forward in your destiny, count on pushback, expect to be challenged, anticipate resistance, wait for questions or accusations. Jesus said to Peter, "Get behind me Satan!" Even He encountered it! You're in good company.

_____

_____

_____

_____

I have made many decisions I wouldn't want to live over again. BUT, I say I can live with the decisions I make (or have made). I can't live with decisions others make for me. Do you have decisions you need to make?

_____

_____

_____

_____

Do you see a vision you need to take action on to make it a reality?

_____

_____

_____

_____

A man without a vision perishes.

Look up: Prov. 29:18, Philippians 4:11, II Timothy 1:7, Colossians 3:2, John 15:18, Matthew 16:23

What is *YOUR* **"Stone of Remembrance?"**

_____

_____

_____

_____

PART 16, DAY 16

Serving is greatness

"The measure of a man's greatness is not the number of servants he has, but the number of people he serves."

JOHN HAGEE | PASTOR & AUTHOR

Few people just "arrive" at the top of the mountain without having to start at the bottom. People can pay their way to get to the top. Most of us can't do that. But I always wonder how they handle "that position" not "paying" the price, not going through the mud, not being broken and rebuilt.

I have a saying; Brokenness is the forgotten factor of Prayer.

The novice (new believer) who jumps into the ministry too soon because they are self-appointed or man appointed versus God appointed can be dangerous to others. How sad.

There are great (lifesaving) benefits to cracking your own "shell" open, breaking out of your own cocoon, or climbing your own mountain!

What's yours? A great time of growth in a great time of struggle?

_____

_____

Struggles build strength, honor, gratitude, empathy, sympathy, insight, and many other internal gems. What character quality do you have NOW that didn't exist before you ascended your "difficult mountain?"

_____

_____

_____

_____

_____

_____

What happen to you as you climbed "that mountain?" Slips? Falls? Stumbles? Broken wings or hearts? Starvation? Thirst? What were important lessons YOU discovered that came out of that "walk" in the forest, UP the mountain?

_____

_____

_____

_____

Do you struggle with unbelief despite what you know is undoubtably His hand that provided? Did you have to cling to fear to climb over the bridge?

_____

_____

_____

_____

Join the club, most of us do, or have. The enemy would love for you to think you're alone. Isolation is key to taking over the lamb.

Think about who you met going up, coming down, or wandering around your own mountain. What influence did they have on your life? What lessons did you learn from them?

_____

_____

_____

_____

One thing I've learned about myself is I LOVE to build. I love to help others build their businesses, and I'm excellent at putting policies and procedures into place. I'm also a great hound dog and can figure out quickly who the troublemaker is in the office. I wish I had the time to start an undercover office agent business to help save businesses money from losing good employees.

Well, on with my Goldie speech . . . But why? Why do we keep getting ourselves stuck in the mud? Just because I love to build doesn't mean I'm a great C.O.O. (Chief Operating Officer) There is nothing wrong being an Indian versus a Chief. A Janitor versus a Receptionist. ***Stop competing and start completing each other!***

_____

_____

_____

_____

Don't forget YOUR mission.

Let's be busy about our Father's business. Follow Him. Not Them. **Look up:** Psalm 37: 23-24, Psalm 23: 5-6, Proverbs 11:3, Isaiah 40:31, Psalm 56:13

What is *YOUR **"Stone of Remembrance?"***

_____

_____

_____

_____

PART 17, DAY 17

Grace sustains us

"The will of God will not take us where the
grace of God will not sustain us."
BILLY GRAHAM | AMERICA'S PASTOR

You're in good company if you have ever realized that the things you don't want to do, you do . . . and the things you do want to do, you don't. The Apostle Paul said that very thing. It's really a mind twister to read it, isn't it?!

Habits and hang-ups can be the "foxes that spoil the vine" keep-on-keeping-on. Turn and repent and get back on the path! God will always offer a way out, look for it! Do you have a habit or hang-up you need to give up?

_____

_____

_____

_____

The Lord gave me the "Highway of Life Directions" a long time ago for good reason. I got "lost" or distracted in the mountain of life. He knew it was going to be a long journey of developing for me that was filled with a forest of blunders and swinging ropes, crowded paths, and dead ends. I took a long time to mature (in my eyes) spiritually (from the bad choices I made), and I'm still sprouting daily.

Life is a "busy forest" with lots of dangers lurking, temptations, curves, and rocky roads. We will all encounter them (if we leave our homes and mingle at all). It's not important that you NOT meet them, what's important is how you respond when you do or upon realizing you've fallen.

Have you ever been on a path, doing well, and then BAM . . . something catches your attention and off the path you go? What was it, how did that happen? Please don't remain in shame or guilt. We are human, this is a training camp for a much longer journey—Eternity.

_____

_____

_____

_____

_____

Where are you today?

_____

_____

_____

_____

I have often wished I could buy hindsight! However, I probably couldn't afford it, because it's truly priceless!

But then, that is one reason I'm an advocate for having mentors. If you accessed your hindsight, would you say you had a way out of most "bad choices?"

_____

_____

_____

_____

Even if it was a "check" in my heart, I can say I had a way out. Somehow, someway, I didn't listen or heed. What about you? Site examples and what you can learn from them to do different "next time."

_____

_____

_____

_____

I heard this grand story from a father recently about how his son became tired of listening to his advice (he was laughing) and met another gentleman that ended up mentoring him in business. It was a great story. When I repeated it to someone briefly he said, _oh no, he is a smart man, he doesn't need mentors._

Huh?

Smart doesn't equal NOT needing mentors. Smart people seek mentors! They join roundtables and exchange lessons and ideas. They realize they DON'T know it all. They understand the value of hindsight and lessons learned.

I had a Pastor once that said he looked for those who had lots of failures to be God's chosen and most successful. Well, I'm raising my hand and thinking **WOW, I have a chance after all!**

Since then, I've had even more falls, even more mistakes, I've messed up so badly and gotten so far behind I'm not sure I'll ever "catch up." I've done so many wrong things, I should be disqualified altogether.

But God's Grace.

I pour myself a new cup of Mercy every day!

First thing in the morning before my feet hit the floor.

I need those Highway of Life Directions.

Now, let me find my glasses to review that . . .

People in the church aren't perfect, just forgiven. No matter how someone tries to act. Your tidy little dress or jacket and tie don't make you clean on the inside! You being an elder doesn't make you better than the widow who can't walk, or orphan who can't read, or the beggar that counts on others for food. Deacon only means servant. Are you the biggest servant in the church? Community?

I had 3 former prostitutes live with me at different times. The lady's in the church were so glad they were with me because "I knew how to dress" (oh really, suddenly they approved?). They told me how wonderful it was I'd teach them . . . tell them their nails were too long, skirts were too short, and their shoes were too chunky versus "lady-like."

Really?

That never entered my mind!

They started to thank me for allowing them to share their ideas when I told them I was on my way to Home Depot™ for a red light and said, "Want one for your porch?"

I told my Pastor if those ladies didn't leave me alone about those girls I was buying a convertible and having a custom bumper sticker made that says, "You outta see me with my top down!"

He died laughing and said, "***You would!*** I'm going to tell them to back off right now!"

One of those dear women sobbed while pouring her heart out to me saying she could never be forgiven. God couldn't forgive her, she couldn't forgive herself, her children wouldn't forgive her—this went on and on *for hours.*

Then I said, "Hey! You're an Entrepreneur!"

She said, "WHAT? @#."

I said, "Yeah … at least you charged for it, most of the ladies just give it away! Well, I shouldn't point fingers at them … I know I have!"

Both of us rolled on the floor laughing.

She forgave herself and went onto marry a street minister.

She died clean, drug-free, and Christian while serving a meal to friends.

That would not have happened if I had harped on "how she should be." I let God himself convict her in HIS timing, in His way … not mine. We need to get out of the way and let God be God to people.

He hasn't hired any of us to be his *Holy* Personal Assistant. He's got a full staff of heavenly hosts!

You're wondering about the other two? One wanted to go back to the streets. It's all she knew, and she missed all she identified with. She was killed one week later. I was so grieved, but we all have choices to make. The other stayed clean and off the streets and was restored to her children last I knew.

Now . . . what "bad choices" have you made that are "unforgiveable?" Do you really think Christ died for everything BUT YOUR ONE THING? Nah.

_____

_____

_____

_____

Look up: Romans 7:15, John 15:16, Song of Songs 2:15, John 15:1, I Corinthians 10:13

What is *YOUR **"Stone of Remembrance?"***

_____

_____

_____

_____

PART 18, DAY 18

Your time is limited

"Your time is limited, so don't waste it living someone else's life. Don't be trapped by dogma — which is living with the results of other people's thinking.
Don't let the noise of others' opinions drown out your own inner voice. And most important, have the courage to follow your heart and intuition."

STEVE JOBS | ENTREPRENEUR

What are your strengths and weaknesses?

Strengths:

_____

_____

_____

Weaknesses:

_____

_____

_____

This is hard for most people to answer. I was always surprised in interviewing adults how many people don't know when asked. It always told me this was a person that didn't do much self-examination. Which could be a plus, because I've always been on the other end of the spectrum. Perhaps others don't think they have weaknesses or don't know how to define them.

Hint: I have found many of my own weaknesses are a negative reflection of my strengths.

For instance:

You might be a giver (strength), but give before asked, give too much, or are convinced you always must give. Perhaps you lean on enabling versus giving in an emotionally healthy manner.

You might be a natural "servant" (strength), but you volunteer so much and resent others for not taking part, or you're always volunteering for the next activity. Well, if they can count on you doing everything, why should they?

Maybe you're very considerate and thoughtful (strength) but to a fault. Don't let people take advantage of you. They can't do it if YOU don't let them. Not people, not the church (you aren't the only one who can serve), not family, friends, or co-workers. Take a seat sometimes and let others jump in to help. See WHO you're fellowshipping. That might be interesting!

How can you work on something you aren't aware of?

Do you have "an eagle" in your life (AKA: mentor) that can teach you how to soar?

_____

_____

_____

Encourage you to, be you?

_____

_____

To fly as high as God created you to? Are you willing to find one?

_____

_____

_____

Who comes to mind?

_____

_____

_____

Think back on a time when you KNOW you shouldn't have done something but because you did it anyway, you had a "bad" consequence play out. That was your discernment at work. That is the Holy Spirit taping on your shoulder saying, "don't do that, don't open that door, don't go down that road."

Think about something recent that happened and you knew that you knew, but you didn't listen. It doesn't have to be a major life event or lifesaving situation. What will you do NEXT TIME you have that sense?

_____

_____

_____

_____

Don't wait for the train to run you over. Listen for the sound coming down the tracks LONG before it hits you. You don't want to be ON the tracks to confirm you were right. I want you to make it to the top of the mountain. To get there before the next 40 years (Moses), LISTEN. You were born to soar!

Look up: Philippians 2:12 (note salvation means deliverance—working on issues), Proverbs 27:17, II Timothy 2:2, Titus 2:3, Psalm 119:130, Proverbs 13:20

What is *YOUR* ***"Stone of Remembrance?"***

_____

_____

_____

_____

PART 19, DAY 19

Reaching Your Destiny... It's a Journey!
There is an eagle in YOU!

"There is an eagle in me that wants to soar, and there is a hippopotamus in me that wants to wallow in the mud."

CARL SANDBURG | POET

Can you laugh about things that happened in the past?

_____

_____

_____

_____

_____

Can you laugh at yourself or do you take yourself very seriously?

_____

_____

_____

_____

I have friends that have told me for years "Bekah, you laugh at stuff other people would cry about!"

My husband and I make "skits up" (not elaborate just funny things between us), and we laugh so hard we're crying. It's better than the Mollie-grubs. It's easier to forgive and move on, it puts things in perspective, and it's fun!

Throw your hands up in the air and speak out loud how many things you're thankful for! I always say, "I'm soooooooo grateful for this trial and tribulation! Woohoo! I'm trusted with this!"

Try it and move on. Don't waste your valuable time sulking or being mad. NO ONE ever woke up in the morning, turned off their alarm, and said, "I will HATE today." MOST people start out unforgiving, then it leads to being frustrated, then mad, which will lead to bitterness, bitterness will lead to anger, and anger will lead to hate. Hate can lead to murder! Yep, I imagine that is why the Bible says, *"hate is as the sin of murder."* Most people who murder are known to have anger and hate issues.

Don't let the sun go down on YOUR wrath.

Forgive . . .

God doesn't call the equipped, he equips the called! 1 Cor. 1:27-29

What do you need to leave in the past in order to focus on the future?

_____

_____

_____

_____

We can only work on ourselves, not others.

Give God a chance, he's given you many.

Build bridges, not walls!

That is . . . The ~~End~~ Beginning!

Look up: Genesis 1:27, Colossians 4:6, Hebrews 13:20-21, Philippians 3:12-14, Ephesians 4:26, Proverbs 4:20-27, John 3:16.

What is *YOUR "Stone of Remembrance?"*

_____

_____

_____

_____

I hope you see how long "Nissi" has been there for you even if you haven't recognized Him. He loves you, and His patience endures forever. His mercy is new every day!

 May God's face shine upon you.

Let Him be the Author and Finisher of *your* story,

Rebekah

> "We must be ready to allow ourselves
> to be interrupted by God."
> DIETRICH BONHOEFFER
> ANTI-NAZI THEOLOGIAN AND PASTOR

If you do not know Jesus Christ as your savior

I want you to have a prayer of salvation, but first there are a few things you should know. There is not an official prayer listed in scripture. It is implied and comes from Romans 10-9-10, "That if thou shalt confess with thy mouth the Lord Jesus, and shalt believe in thine heart that God hath raised him from the dead, thou shalt be saved. For with the heart man believeth unto righteousness; and with the mouth confession is made unto salvation." I have put *my heart* down in ink for you to read a prayer of salvation.

Second, I want you to know that repentance means you are *turning* to God and you are having *faith* and *trust* that Christ will be true to HIS Word and forgive you. HE WILL meet you where you are. Remember: Grace doesn't give us an excuse to continue in our sin or harbor un-forgiveness. True repentance brings change and the desire to *turn* from the old things and embrace the new. You are willfully laying down *your will* for HIS. You are accepting that Jesus Christ IS the Son of God. If you run into something difficult (like forgiving someone) ASK The Lord to help you, ask HIM to give you the desire to do so and remember, no one has done anything to us that we haven't done to HIM. At the end of the day, our sin is against HIM and HIM only.

Last, your walk doesn't *end* with a prayer (unless you're literally on your death bed). *It begins at this point*. I'm assigning *homework* ... Now, find a good, solid, Bible- based church and get a foundation laid. Read the Gospels (Matthew, Mark, Luke and John) to learn who Jesus is and what he expects from you as his adopted son/daughter. Get baptized. It is an act of obedience and a public acknowledgment of HIM. Get a Bible if you don't have one, and above all *be a doer* of what you learn.

You may not feel any difference immediately (some do, some don't), but HE is at work in you, so take the next steps of your journey. I look forward to meeting you in heaven, if not before.

Welcome to the family of God, I'm rejoicing with heaven ...

Your sister 'in Christ,'

Rebekah

PS: *You may not know, but ALL of Heaven rejoices over one sinner coming to the Lord. (Luke 15:10) Isn't that an amazing thought to ponder?*

PRAYER OF SALVATION

My *Father*, in heaven, I recognize you as *my* sovereign God, the creator of the universe to the creator of my heart. Who knew me before I was even in my mother's womb.

I am coming to you, to acknowledge your son, *Jesus Christ* as my savior who came to die for my sins. Forgive me that it took me so long to humble myself to come to you. Forgive me of my selfish pride; forgive me of all my sins, Father, known and unknown. I want your son to be my Lord and savior, and I welcome him to be my friend and teacher. I'm grateful you made Christ the way, the truth and the light, rather than me having to live by law(s), by sacrifices, and in eternal darkness away from you. I recognize, by faith, HE became the sacrifice. Teach me your ways, Lord, guide my feet to the straight and narrow path you laid out for me to take. Redeem the time I have lived without you Lord and teach me how to use my life for your will and your purposes, until you return, no matter the cost. Put a watch over me, Lord, and encompass me with strength when I am faced with my weaknesses. HELP me to flee temptations and see the way of escape that you will provide. Thank you, Jesus, for coming into my life and changing *me* to reflect *you*!

Amen. So be it and Let it be so.

ABOUT THE AUTHOR

Rebekah Phelps is the Poet behind "The Psalm of my Heart," a prayer that the Lord gave to her, which she attributes as a Psalm. It is a Psalm to *the follower,* stating who we are IN Christ.

From 2005 to 2015, Rebekah founded and managed two personal services companies, Extra You and White House Home Inventory. Her businesses served The DC Metro area and The Eastern Panhandle of West Virginia. In addition, she worked for eight years as a hospice volunteer, and assisted adults with autism and Down syndrome.

Her vision for *I'm an Eagle, not a Field Chick* began in 2009, and came to fruition in 2015. She has a vision for a "family book. She is currently developing additional versions for children and toddlers, along with a block book for infants. She has also created an adult puzzle of the first edition cover. Rebekah has been happily married to George Phelps since 2004. They enjoy traveling extensively in their RV and make their home (6 months out of the year) in Florida.

Contact the author via her website, www.rebekahleaphelps.com.

STAY IN TOUCH

The Author, Rebekah, would love to have your feedback and hear from you. You may go to her website and download a piece of *I'm an Eagle, not a Field Chick* stationary or visit her website at www.RebekahLeaPhelps.com and join her mailing list!

Rebekah Lea Phelps, Speaker and Author

Would you like to work together, Keep in touch?

I speak, would you like to listen?

I am available for workshops, as a group or with a book club. Speaking topics are from first-hand experience. Topic can be centered around the book, a chapter, or one of the following below. If something isn't listed and you'd like to know if I can talk about it, give me a call. If I can't, I'll help you find someone who can!

Speaking Topics

The journey of discovering who you are

How to use or recognize your gifts and talents

Identity in Christ

Prayer – Knowing who you are

Setting healthy boundaries

So now you're a caregiver

Parent versus a Pal

Mental illness in adult children | Tough love

Grief | PTSD – Finding your way back

Renewing your mind | Detox your brain

Getting rid of stink'in thinkin'

Speaking To:

Churches, women's study groups

Home groups and associations

Business groups | Lunch and learn

Cancer groups | Cancer gene | Choices

Parent groups | Not losing who you are

Alzheimer's | Dementia Groups

Hospitals, rehabs, support groups

Schools

Prisons, male or female

Bookstores | Libraries

Webinars | Skype | GoToMeetings

Spiritual abuse – being battered w/o physical bruises

Divorce and the Church – the shame

Homeless adult children

Lessons in life

Courage to be who you were born to be

What happens to your identity when it's gone? Loss of children, health, spouse

Grief Recovery. Certified to teach.

Walking through the workbook together!

WAYS TO CONNECT

Rebekah Lea Phelps | RebekahLeaPhelps@Gmail.com | RebekahLeaPhelps.com

Sign up for a Newsletter on website www.RebekahLeaPhelps.com

Email: RebekahLeaPhelps@Gmail.com | 832-953-4742

SOCIAL MEDIA - FOLLOW ME FOR:

My quotes, inspiration, life lessons, artwork, recipes

Instagram rebekahleaphelps_author   Rebekah Lea Phelps | Author

What I PIN, decorating ideas, my quotes, my taste

Pinterest Pinterest.com/RebekahLeaPhelps   Rebekah Lea Phelps | Speaker

LIKE my Facebook Business Page. Inspirational Stories, my quotes, testimonies

Facebook facebook.com/RebekahPhelpsBooks   @RebekahPhelpsBooks

Don't use LinkedIn much, but when I do, it's about events, business tips, video, blog

LinkedIn linkedin.com/in/RebekahaLeaPhelps   Rebekah Lea Phelps

My Goofball Self

Snapchat Rebekah Phelps   bekahleaphelps

Rants, speaking out, speaking up

Twitter twitter.com/RebekahLPhelps   @RebekahLPhelps

Educational, thoughts, elaborating on my books, life lessons, live examples

YouTube youtube.com/RebekahLeaPhelps   SUBSCRIBE!

Made in United States
Orlando, FL
03 April 2022

16438114R00128